E-LEADERSHIP

E-LEADERSHIP

A New Paradigm

Dr. Monika Bansal

GYAN

The publication was financially supported by the ICSSR. The responsibility for the facts stated, opinions expressed, or conclusions reached, is entirely that of the author and that the ICSSR accepts no responsibility for them.

Consultant: Professor S.K. Singh, Faculty of Management Studies, Banaras Hindu University (B.H.U.), Varanasi.

E-Leadership: A New Paradigm

ISBN: 978-81-212-1064-5

Published in 2010 in India by
Gyan Publishing House,
23, Main Ansari Road, Darya Ganj,
New Delhi-110002
Ph.: 23282060, 23261060
Fax: 011-23285914
E-mail: books@gyanbooks.com
Website: www.gyanbooks.com
Laser Typesetting at: Square Vision, Delhi
Printed at: Chawla Offset Printers, Delhi

CONTENTS

LIST OF TABLES

LIST OF CHARTS

LIST OF FIGURES

FOREWORD

In 1789 Ben Franklin wrote to a friend, "But in this world nothing is certain but death and taxes." He neglected to mention a third certainty: Change. Change have been, are, and will continue to be an ever present features of our life. The process of life itself is continuous change.

Business organizations are continuously changing. An organization has to operate in a dynamic socio-political-techno-economic environment. Any change in the external environment requires that appropriate changes be made within the organization. The objectives, strategies, policies, structure, personnel, leadership and methods of operations of the organization must change so that it can become or remain financially sound and socially responsible.

The time today has arrived for us to identify it as an electronic age or simply the e-age. The alphabet "e" has brought in the concept of electronically managing different facets of our lives. It has not only impacted the infrastructure, modes of operation, technical expertise but also has influenced the human capital of the organization. The impact of this "e" factor is felt in the domain of leadership as well.

Leaders in today's business world need to grapple with two interrelated issues. The work of leaders in organization has become highly global. The components of the organization in the form of divisions, customers, stakeholders and suppliers are often extended worldwide. Secondly because of the exponential growth of information technology there is a greater frequency of daily interaction between colleagues, coworker, bosses and subordinates. They stay in touch with each other through telephones, overnight express mail, fax-machines and groupware tools such as e-mail, bulletin boards, chats and video conferencing.

Leadership in the electronic age is definitely going to be different. As the impressive and seemingly constant parade of developments in computer and the communication technology continuous to change our world, it has to be assessed as to what has remained the same and what has changed. One important aspect of organizational life which is undergoing tremendous change is the context of leadership which is emerging as e-leadership. It might be true that we are using the advanced information technology to lead and to follow without necessarily knowing the full extent of its impact on human dynamics in organizations. We need to inquire whether it is working or not?

In an organizational set-up the way people approach and react to each other is undergoing tremendous change. The old life style of the business organization has been overshadowed by the impact of information technology. When you do not get to see your bosses, your subordinates or colleagues physically, a totally different approach in terms of strategy and methods of interaction with them is required. This is the impact of e-age on employees. In the absence of physical presence of their leaders there is an impact on their behavior, thinking, efficiency, performance, motivation and satisfaction. This will have serious implications for leaders and followers in teams and organizations where interactions are modified by information technology. The impact of the factor "e" on the level of trust, motivation, commitment and performance of the employees has to be given a new look and new paradigm.

According to e-business consultant Eric Marcus, the technology represents only 5 percent of the change process. The rest 95% of the transformation are all about changes in the behavior of the people and culture of the organization that are heart of e-leadership. E-leaders have to create an environment where everyone unleashes their creativity in the absence of leader. Not an easy task indeed!! It will require trusting employees to work independently in scattered offices. The leaders will have to give up their hierarchical status, line of authority and even the physical space.

With the scarcity of research in the area of e-leadership, especially in a developing economy like India, the present book would act initially as a starting point and later as a benchmark for future researchers, practitioners, educators, employees and leaders as they need to understand and master the skills of dealing with the present changes in the organizational systems and processes. I think this book will be a useful addition in the area of e-leadership and Indian students who are also the future leaders will particularly find it useful.

Dr. Kavita Singh
Faculty of Management Studies
University of Delhi - 110007

PREFACE

Time has certainly arrived, when we can call the present age as the electronic age or as popular, the e-age. This e-age has added an 'e' to virtually everything we see in the present time. But the difference is in the meaning that gets added, which depends on the context. Here, we are going to talk about the impact of this 'e' factor on the simple phenomenon of leadership in business organizations. How does this 'e' actually make the difference when added to leadership making it e-leadership?

Having the Information Technology shadowed the old life style; a major change can be noticed in the way people work or are required to work. In the working environment, where you do not get to see your employees or team members daily or not at all it requires different approach, different strategy and different methods to interact with them. The similar change in turn, of course reflects in their behavior, their thinking, their efficiency, their performance, their motivation, their satisfaction etc. It becomes essential to track this effect so as to mould the current practices, if all the resources are to be put to the best use. This is no new idea, but the divulging of the old basic law of 'adaptation to the change to survive', the only difference being that the change is not so manifest, as it is gradual and abstract in nature.

But the question arises what are the implications for leaders and followers in teams and organizations where interactions are now mediated by information technology? How should we develop leaders to work in this new environment? How does the technology affect trust, motivation, commitment and performance levels? What does "having a presence," mean when the leader is projected into the work group via technology? And what will organizations look like when we move through this time period and fully implement e-leadership, teams & organizations?

In this context, the study is focused to identify the impact of physical absence of leader in IT organizations i.e., where he is in touch with his team members through IT mediated ways and vice versa. Various measures used in the study include Motivation, Trust, Commitment, Organizational Culture, and Performance and a set of objectives and hypotheses were formulated.

In the present study an attempt has been made to study e-leadership in business organizations. The idea was to do a comparative analysis i.e., Traditional Leadership vis-à-vis E-Leadership: A Comparative Analysis of Business Organizations.

ACKNOWLEDGEMENTS

I am regardfully indebted to Dr. Kavita Singh, who has given her valuable time in supervising my research and guiding me in bringing it up to the mark out of her specialized knowledge in the field of Organisational Behavior. But for her consistent interest, inspiring supervision, thoughtful advice, and constructive criticism, this research would not have taken its present shape.

I owe my thanks to Prof. C D Bhattacharya, Prof. M.L Singla and Dr. Mala Sinha for their kind support and availability.

I sincerely thank late Prof. A K Seth for his constant inspiration. I also take the opportunity to thank Prof. Sri Ram Khanna for his valuable suggestions and timely help in completing the study.

My words, in any form, will not suffice to express my feelings of gratitude and regard for my respected parents, my brother Deepak Bansal and sister Sonika Bansal; who are largely responsible for the successful completion of this work. I deeply acknowledge their untiring efforts in giving me motivation, strength and all material and moral support. Without constant efforts and persuasion of my husband Sonu Garg this research work could not have been published as a book. And I don't want to diminish his concerns for me by thanking him.

I am indeed, thankful to all my friends and colleagues who helped and encouraged me to keep the pace specially Dr. Garima Gupta and Ms. Abha Shukla.

In the end, I wish to record my gratitude to all those who have, directly or indirectly, helped me.

1 INTRODUCTION

1.1 Introduction

The global economy is undergoing a major transition with the advancements in the Information Technology. The rapid advances in information and communication technology which allow people to more easily generate, organize, and access information have real implications for the capacities that leaders need. New technology has the potential to affect the distribution of power and the development of relationships in organizations. Therefore, an Information Technology enabled economy is creating a new context for leadership and it becomes important to consider how Information Technology interacts with leadership to influence both the structure and effects of leadership and how leadership, in turn, might influence the adoption of advanced Information Technology and its effects on organization.

Leaders in today's business world need to grapple with two interrelated forces. First, the work of organizations and leadership has become increasingly global. An organization's divisions and subunits, customers, stakeholders, and suppliers can often extend worldwide. Second, the exponential explosion in communicating technology has resulted in greater frequency of daily interactions with colleagues, coworkers, subordinates and bosses who are dispersed in different geographic locations. Today, business leaders typically lead teams in which members are located, not in the same office or building, but in different places around the world. Many leaders and team members stay in contact with each other by interacting through telephone, overnight express mail, fax-machine and groupware tools such as e-mail, bulletin boards, chat and video conferencing.

In response to these changes people have begun to talk about e-leadership to refer to leaders who conduct many of the processes of leadership largely through electronic channels.

Leadership in the electronic age is surely different. As the impressive and seemingly constant parade of developments in computer and communications technology continues to change our world, we ask what remains the same and what has changed. One tremendously important context for leadership is impact of e-factor on leadership.

It is different because it alters the patterns of how information is acquired, stored, interpreted and disseminated and that, in turn, alters how people are influenced and how decisions are made in organizations. The following are some specific happenings brought about by information technology in a way that alters leadership and its bases of power:

1. Access to information and media has changed.
2. Greater workforce inter-connectedness.
3. It is easier to reach and touch others.
4. Communication is more indelible than before.

E-leadership can be defined as a social influence process mediated by information technology to produce a change in attitudes, feelings, thinking, behaviour, and/or performance with individuals, groups, and/or organizations. (Avolio, Kahai, and Dodge, 2001).

The key difference between leadership and e-leadership is that e-leadership takes place in a context where work is mediated by information technology. In such a context, not only may a leader's communication with followers take place via information technology, but the collection and dissemination of information required to support organizational work also takes place via information technology. The critical differences may be in what is meant by "feeling the leader's presence", as well as reach, speed, permanence, and perception of a leader's communication. But the purpose of e-leadership too is to take the relationship among organizational members defined by an organization's structure.

The most fundamental bottom line is that e-leadership ultimately is not about connecting technology, but about connecting people.

1.2 Why E-Leadership

Having the Information Technology shadowed the old life style; a major change can be noticed in the way people work or are required to work. In the working environment where you do not get to see your employees or team members daily or not at all, it requires different approach, different strategy and different methods to interact with them. The similar change in turn, of course reflects in their behavior, their thinking, their efficiency, their performance, their motivation, their satisfaction etc. It becomes essential to track this effect so as to mould the current practices, if all the resources are to be put to the best use. This is no new idea, but the divulging of the old basic law of 'adaptation to the change to survive', the only difference being that the change is not so manifest, as it is gradual and abstract in nature.

But the question arises what are the implications for leaders and followers in teams and organizations where interactions are now mediated by information technology? How should we develop leaders to work in this new environment? How does the technology affect trust, motivation, commitment and performance levels? What does "having a presence," mean when the leader is projected into the work group via technology?

As is true that we are using and investing in advanced information technology to lead and to follow with an anticipation of increased profits, improved efficiency with enhanced productivity without necessarily knowing the full extent of its impact on human dynamics in organizations. Is it really working?

Likewise there are many issues which are needed to be explored as e-leadership is in its infancy stage. A whole new area is open for the research.

Since no such kind of research has been carried out in past in the Indian context, therefore an attempt has been made to do an empirical study on the issue of e-leadership.

In this context, the research is focused to identify the impact of physical absence of leader in organizations i.e., where he is in touch with his team members through IT mediated ways and vice versa. Various measures used in the study include Motivation, Trust, Commitment, Organizational Culture, and Performance. A set of objectives and hypotheses have been formulated.

1.3 Issues of Concern

Keeping in mind the studies which have been carried out in past on the issue of leadership and e-leadership, it has been found that there are many areas of concern which are affected by the phenomenon of leadership/ e-leadership, for example, Perception, Motivation, Learning, Trust, Attribution, Organizational Culture, Commitment, Conflict, Performance etc. Out of these concepts some are largely influenced by leadership/e-leadership as compared to others. After a close review of these concepts some of the dimensions based on their importance to the organizations were chosen for the study. These dimensions are Motivation, Trust, Commitment, Organizational Culture and Performance.

The main objective of the study was to have a comparative analysis of business organization with traditional leadership vis-à-vis e-leadership based on various dimensions like:

- Motivation
- Trust
- Commitment
- Organizational Culture
- Performance

The objectives were further divided into following aspects for proper analysis:

- To compare the effectiveness of traditional leadership and e-leadership on motivation.
- To assess the level of trust among employees in organizations with traditional leadership and e-leadership.
- To study the commitment level of employees in organizations in e-leadership vis-à-vis traditional leadership.
- To see the impact of leadership and e-leadership on organizational culture.
- To assess the performance of organizations with leader-ship and e-leadership.

1.4 Hypotheses for the Research

An exploratory study has been taken to gain insight about the organizations involved in e-leadership and the impact of various dimensions undertaken in the research proposal. A set of hypotheses have been generated to evaluate the impact of leadership and e-leadership on different dimensions.

Hypotheses

1. There is a positive impact of e-leadership on motivation as compared to traditional leadership.
2. E-leadership influence the trust level positively in team members when compared with traditional leadership.

3. There is a favourable bearing of e-leadership on commitment level in leader-follower dynamics as compared to traditional leadership.
4. E-leadership positively influences the organizational culture when compared with traditional leadership.
5. E-leadership plays a positive role in performance of the team members in comparison to traditional leadership.

1.5 The Way to Research

The present research work is an empirical one based on both primary and secondary data. The theory is built from secondary sources of information such as articles and textbooks, and the same have been duly acknowledged at the relevant places. Primary data have been collected with the help of a self-administered questionnaire. Two sectors viz., Business Process Outsourcing (BPO) and Information Technology (IT) have been taken as sample population and a survey of 300 employees in these two sectors from Delhi and NCR region has been conducted to assess the impact of physical absence of leader on the processes of Motivation, Trust, Commitment, Organizational Culture, and Performance. The data so obtained from the survey have been processed and analyzed using SPSS package. Statistical techniques like t-test, correlation and regression analysis, and measures of central tendency have been used in the study.

2 LEADERSHIP AND E-LEADERSHIP: A CONCEPTUAL FRAMEWORK

The following chapter provides a brief description of the concept of leadership along with the explanation of some major theories in the area. A concise note is given on the overall work done in the area of leadership. This is followed by the notion of e-leadership and the review of work carried out on the topic.

2.1 Leadership

Leadership is a subject that has gained increasing interest among scholars. The term connotes images of powerful, dynamic individuals who command victorious armies, direct corporate empires from atop or shape the course of nations.

Questions about leadership have long been a subject of speculation, but specific research on leadership did not begin until the twentieth century. The focus of much of the research has been on determinants of leadership effectiveness. Behavioural scientists have attempted to discover what traits, abilities, behaviours, sources of power, or aspects of the situation determine how well a leader is able to influence followers and accomplish group objectives. The reason why some people emerge as leaders and the determinants of the way a leader acts are other important questions that have been investigated but the predominated concern has been leadership effectiveness.

Leadership has been studied in different ways depending on the researcher's methodological preferences and conception of leadership.

Some of the definitions of Leadership given by eminent researchers are:

Stogdill (1974) says that:

"Leadership is the initiation and maintenance of structure in expectation and interaction."

James MacGregor Burns (1978) concedes that:

"Leadership is leaders inducing followers to act for certain goals that represent the values and the motivations – 'the wants and needs, the aspirations and expectations' - of both leaders and followers. And the genius of leadership lies in the manner in which leaders see and act on their own and their followers' values and motivations."

According to Katz and Kahn (1978):

"Leadership is the influential increment over and above mechanical compliance with the routine directives of the organization."

According to John Gardner (1990):

"Leadership is the process of persuasion and example by which an individual (or leadership team) induces a group to take action that is in accord with the leader's purpose or the shared purposes of all."

Buchannan and Huczynski (1997) explain leadership as:

"A social process in which one individual influences the behaviour of others without the use of threat or violence."

Most researchers deal with only one narrow aspect of leadership and most of the studies fall into distinct lines of research. As shown in Figure 2.1, most leadership research can be classified into one of the following approaches:

1. Trait Approach
2. Behavioural Approach
3. Contingency Theories
4. Contemporary Approaches

2.1.1 Theories of Leadership

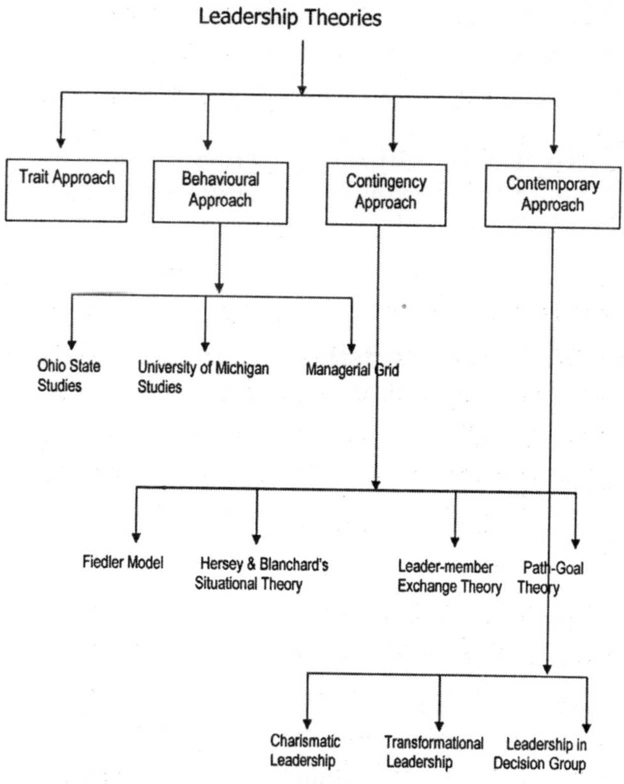

Figure: 2.1. Classification of Major Leadership Theories

Trait Approach

One of the earliest approaches for studying leadership was the trait approach. These theories sought personality, social, physical, or intellectual traits that differentiated leaders from non leaders. Underlying this approach was the assumption that some people are natural leaders who are endowed with certain traits not possessed by other people. Early leadership theories attributed managerial success to possession of extraordinary abilities such as tireless energy, penetrating intuition, uncanny foresight, and irresistible persuasive powers. Hundreds of trait studies were conducted during the 1930s and 1940s to discover these elusive qualities, but this massive research effort failed to find any traits that would guarantee leadership success. Some of the traits identified were as following:

Personality traits: self-confident, adaptable, assertive, emotionally stable etc.

Task-related characteristics: driven to excel, accepting of responsibility, having initiative, results-oriented etc.

Physical traits: young to middle-aged, energetic, tall, handsome etc.

Social characteristics: charismatic, charming, tactful, popular, cooperative, diplomatic etc.

But the trait approach failed to predict universal set of traits that predict leadership in all situations. Rather, traits appear to predict leadership in selective situations.

Behavioural Approach

In the 1950s when researchers became discouraged with the trait approach, they began to pay closer attention to what managers actually do on the job. Researchers started to look at the behaviors that specific leaders exhibited. They developed training programs to change managers' leadership behaviors and assumed that the best styles of leadership could be learned.

Some of the major theories of Behaviour approach have been discussed here briefly.

Ohio State Studies

The most comprehensive and replicated behavioral theories result from research that began at Ohio State University in the late 1940s. These researchers sought to identify independent dimensions of leader behavior. The Ohio State study identified two leadership styles: initiating and considerate structure.

Initiating structure refers to the extent to which a leader is likely to define and structure his or her role and those of employees in the search for goal attainment.

Consideration is described as the extent to which a person is likely to have job relationships that are characterized by mutual trust, respect for employees' ideas, and regard for their feelings. He or she shows concern for followers' comfort, well being, status, and satisfaction. It was found that leaders high in initiating structure and consideration (a "high-high leader") tended to achieve high employee performance and satisfaction more frequently than those who rated low on consideration, initiating structure, or both. However, the "high-high" style did not always result in positive consequences.

University of Michigan Studies

The University of Michigan study classified leaders' behaviors as being production oriented and employee-centered. The primary concern of leaders with employee-centered style is the employee's welfare. The primary concern of leaders with production-centered style is achieving goals. However, employee oriented leaders appear to be associated with high group productivity and job satisfaction. Production oriented leaders tended to be associated with low group productivity and lower job satisfaction.

Managerial Grid

The Managerial Grid is a behavioral leadership model

developed by Robert Blake and Jane Mouton in 1964. This model identifies five different leadership style based on the concern for people and the concern for production.

As shown in the Figure 2.2, the model is represented as a grid with concern for production on the X-axis and concern for people on the Y-axis; each axis ranging from 1 (Low) to 9 (High). The five resulting leadership styles are as follows:

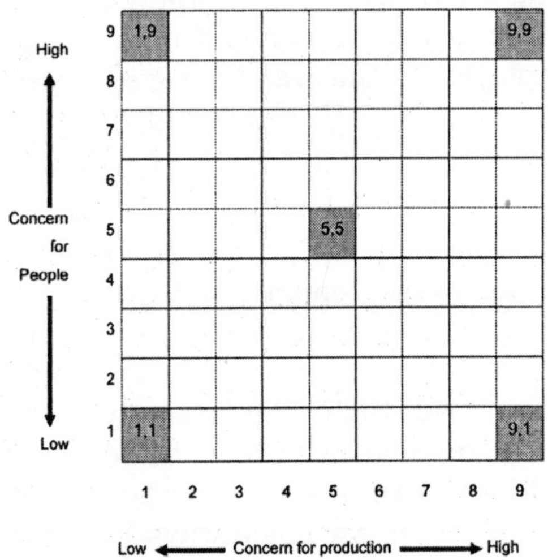

Figure: 2.2 Managerial Grid.

The Impoverished Style (1, 1)

In this style, managers have low concern for both people and production. Managers use this style to avoid getting into trouble. The main concern for the manager is not to be held responsible for any mistakes, which results in less innovative decisions.

The Country Club Style (1, 9)

This style has a high concern for people and a low concern for production. Managers using this style pay much attention to the security and comfort of the employees, in the hope that this would increase performance. The resulting atmosphere is usually friendly, but not necessarily productive.

The Produce or Perish Style (9, 1)

With a high concern for production and a low concern for people, this style find employee needs unimportant. The managers provide their employees with money and expect performance back. Managers using this style also pressurize their employees through rules and punishments to achieve the company goals. This dictatorial style is based on Theory X and is commonly applied by companies on the edge of real or perceived failure.

The Middle-of-the-road Style (5, 5)

Managers using this style try to balance between company goals and workers' needs. By giving some concern to both people and production, managers who use this style hope to achieve acceptable performance.

The Team Style (9, 9)

In this style, high concern is paid both to people and production. As suggested by the propositions of Theory Y, managers choosing this style encourage teamwork and commitment among employees. This method relies heavily on making employees feel as a constructive part of the company.

Contingency Theories

In this theory, the success of the leader is a function of various factors in the form of subordinate, task, and/ or group variables. The effectiveness of a given pattern of leader behaviour is contingent upon the demands imposed by the situation. These theories stress using different styles of leadership appropriate to the needs created by different organizational situations. Some of these theories are:

- Fiedler's Contingency Model
- Hersey-Blanchard Situational Theory
- Path-Goal Theory
- Leader-Member Exchange Theory

Fiedler's Contingency Model

Fiedler's theory is the earliest and most extensively researched. Fiedler's approach departs from trait and behavioural models by asserting that group performance is contingent on the leader's psychological orientation and on three contextual variables: group atmosphere, task structure, and leader's power position.

Fiedler's model assumes that group performance depends on

➢ Leadership style

➢ Situational favourableness, determined by three factors viz.,

  - Leader-member relations i.e. the degree to which a leader is accepted and supported by the group members.
  - Task structure i.e. the extent to which the task is structured and defined, with clear goals and procedures.
  - Position power i.e. the ability of a leader to control subordinates through reward and punishment.

While the high levels of these three factors give the most favourable situation, low levels generate the least favourable situation. Relationship-motivated leaders are most effective in moderately favourable situations. Task-motivated leaders are most effective at either end of the scale.

Fiedler suggests that it may be easier for leaders to change their situation to achieve effectiveness rather than change their leadership style.

Hersey-Blanchard Situational Theory

This theory suggests that leadership style should be matched to the maturity of the subordinates. Maturity is assessed in relation to a specific task and has two parts:

- Psychological maturity, which reflects their self-confidence, ability and readiness to accept responsibility.
- Job maturity, which reflects their relevant skills and technical knowledge.

As the subordinate maturity increases, leadership should be more relationship-motivated than task-motivated. For four degrees of subordinate maturity, from highly mature to highly immature, leadership can consist of:

- Delegating to subordinates.
- Participating with subordinates.
- Selling ideas to subordinates.
- Telling subordinates what to do

Path-Goal Theory

Evans and House suggest that the performance, satisfaction and motivation of a group can be affected by the leader in a number of ways:

- Offering rewards for the achievement of performance goals.
- Clarifying paths towards these goals.
- Removing performance obstacles.

A person may do these by adopting a certain leadership style according to the situation:

- **Directive leadership** - Specific advice is given to the group and ground rules are established.
- **Supportive leadership** - Good relations exist with the group and sensitivity to subordinates' needs is shown.
- **Participative leadership** - Decision making is

based on group consultation and information is shared with the group.

- **Achievement-oriented leadership** - Challenging goals are set and high performance is encouraged while showing confidence in the groups' ability.

Supportive behaviour increases group satisfaction, particularly in stressful situations, while directive behaviour is suited to ambiguous situations. It is also suggested that leaders who have influence upon their superiors can increase group satisfaction and performance.

In contrast to the Fiedler contingency model, the path-goal model states that the four leadership styles are fluid, and that leaders can adopt any of the four depending on what the situation demands.

Leader-Member Exchange Theory

The Leader-member exchange (LMX) theory argues that because of time pressures, leaders establish a special relationship with a small group of their followers. These individuals make up the in-group. They are trusted, get a disproportionate amount of the leader's attention, and are more likely to receive special privileges. Other followers fall into the out-group. They get less of the leader's time, fewer of the preferred rewards that the leader controls, and have leader-follower relations based on formal authority interactions.

Contemporary Approaches

Charismatic and Transformational Leadership

Another line of influence research attempts to explain why the followers of some leaders are willing to exert exceptional effort and make personal sacrifices to accomplish the group objective and mission. The effectiveness of a leader is explained in terms of his/her influence on the way followers view themselves and interprets events. Effective leaders influence followers to have more optimism, self-confidence and commitment to the objectives or mission of the organization. Most theories of charismatic and transformations leadership identify the types of behaviour used by the leader and traits that facilitate the leader's effectiveness. In contrast to other approaches in leadership research, follower perceptions and attributions are also considered to be important for understanding leadership effectiveness. The same behaviour by a leader may have a different effect on followers depending on the current situation, the prior history of interaction between the leaders and the followers and the way the behaviour is interpreted by followers.

Leadership in Decision Group

Much of a manager's time is spent in formal and informal meetings with subordinates, peers, superiors and outsiders. Meetings are held to solve problems, make decisions and coordinate related activities. Many management meetings run too long and fail to result in an agreement because essential leadership functions are not carried out by anyone. What leaders should do to make meetings more effective has been the subject of research by behavioural scientists over the last three decades. Consultants and practitioners have also contributed to our knowledge about leadership in decision groups.

2.1.2 Concluding Leadership

The field of leadership is presently in a state of turmoil and confusion. Most of the leadership theories are beset with conceptual weaknesses and strong lack empirical support. Several empirical studies have been conducted on leadership effectiveness but the results have been found to be contradictory and inconclusive. The confusion in the field is nothing new.

Bennis (1959) made the following observation:

"Of all the hazy and confounding areas in social psychology, leadership theory undoubtedly contends for the top nomination. And, ironically, probably more has been written and less known about leadership than about any other topic in behavioural sciences."

In 1974, after making an extensive review of more than three thousand leadership studies, the following conclusion was reached by Stogdill (1974):

"Four decades of research on leadership have produced a bewildering mass of findings...... The endless accumulation of empirical data has not produced an integrated understand of leadership"

Lombardo and McCall (1978) made the following obser-vations about the leadership literature:

"The number of unintegrated models, theories, prescriptions and conceptual schemes of leadership is mind-boggling.... Much of the literature is fragmentary, trivial, unrealistic or dull."

Salancik, Calder, Rowland, Leblebici and Conway (1975) were even more critical:

"There is perhaps no area of study in organizational behaviour which has more blind alleys and less critical knowledge than the area of leadership. Practitioners and researchers alike have groped for years with such questions as: What is leadership? How does it work? How does one become an effective leader? Yet after many years of investigation, it appears we have no ready useful answers."

Miner (1975) concluded, *"the concept of leadership has outlined its usefulness; and he suggested a moratorium on traditional leadership research."*

The leadership literature currently includes over 5000 studies and the number continues to increase by hundreds each year. The confused state of the field can be attributed in large part to the sheer volume of publications, the disparity of approaches, the proliferation of confusing terms, the narrow focus of most researchers, the high percentage of irrelevant or trivial studies, the preference for simplistic explanations, and the lack of research designed to integrate different aspects of leadership and develop a general theory. As the old adage goes, it is difficult to see the forest for the trees.

Leadership research has been characterized by narrowly focused studies with little integration of findings from different approaches. The trait research has shown little concern for direct measurement of leadership behaviour, even though it is evident that the effects of leader traits on criteria of leadership success are mediated by leadership behaviour. The behaviour research has seldom included leader traits or power, even though they influence a leader's behaviour. Moreover, most behaviour studies do not measure the intervening variables that would explain how leader behaviour affects success criteria. The power influence approach has included some research on influence tactics, but other aspects of leadership behaviour have not been examined in relation to these influence processes. There has been only a relatively small amount of research on the relationship of traits to power and influence. Finally, most situational theories examine how the situation enhances or nullifies the effects of selected leader behaviour or traits, rather than taking a broader view of the way traits, power, behaviour and situation interact to determine leadership effectiveness.

A general theory of leadership that explains all aspects of the process adequately has yet to be developed. However, an integrated conceptual framework was presented to show the likely relationship among major types of variables included in most prior research on leadership.

2.2 E-Leadership

As it has been beautifully imagined by Susan Annunzio (2001) - What if one morning you arrived at your corporate offices and no one was there? The salespeople, equipped with palmtops, thinkpads and mobile phones were operating in mobile virtual offices. Because of economies, customer service had been moved to another city, as had your distribution warehouse. The R & D team you assembled was a collection of brilliant thinkers located around the world who worked with each other on networked computers and the occasional videoconference. Your support staff- accounting, communications, corporate counsel preferred to telecommute, plugging into the network from home offices and talking to each other via email and fax. Even your personal assistant actually was located at the offices of your corporate parent, five hundred miles away, you and he communicated via calendar software, page and overnight mail. What if, sitting alone at a big desk, you realize you didn't need a corporate office building at all? What would you do?

Welcome to the world of e-leadership, where business strategies are fluid, workers are smarter and more demanding than ever, and the old rules of business just don't apply.

It's a world of global markets, adhoc teams, telecommuters, e-mail, videoconferences, online ordering, virtual offices, intranets, networked alliances and instant information. And its full of both challenges and opportunities for e-leaders.

The rapid advances in Information and Communication technology which allows people to more easily generate, organize and access information have real implications for both the capacities that leaders need and the design of developmental experiences.

New technology has the potential to affect the distribution power and the development of relationships in organizations. A number of propositions have been made about these factors and their implications for leadership. Two of the more salient ones are-

1. Greater access to information across the organization has a leveling affect (those in formal leadership roles are no longer the main conduit through which information flows).
2. The sheer volume of accessible information strains a person's ability to make sense of the information (making sense of all these data and their implications for the organization is an increasingly complex leadership task).

Leadership in an Internet economy is about leadership in a connected economy that the personal computers, mobile phones, the PDA and ofcourse, the Internet have made possible. To succeed in a connected economy, each one of us needs to get the heart of leadership and discover the difference between things like sourcing and reacting, between what's possible and what's predictable, between transformation and change. At the same time, each one of us needs to develop the ways of being, mindset and behaviour for succeeding in a connected economy.

2.2.1 The Impact of E-Age

Having the Information Technology shadowed the old life style; a major change can be noticed in the way people work or are required to work. In the working environment, where you do not get to see your employees or team members daily or not at all it requires different approach, different strategy and different methods to interact with them. The similar change in turn, of course reflects in their behavior, their thinking, their efficiency, their performance, their motivation, their satisfaction etc. It becomes essential to track this effect so as to mould the current practices, if all the resources are to be put to the best use. This is no new idea, but the divulging of the old basic law of 'adaptation to the change to survive', the only difference being that the change is not so manifest, as it is gradual and abstract in nature.

Time has certainly arrived when we can call the present age as the electronic age or as popular-- the e-Age. This e-Age has added an 'e' to virtually everything we see in the present time. But the difference is in the meaning that gets added, which depends on the context. Here, we are going to talk about the impact of this 'e' – factor on the simple phenomenon of leadership in business organizations. How does this 'e' actually make the difference when added to leadership making it e-leadership?

Let us first take a look on how do the business environments differ in old industrial age and today's e-Age. Table 2.1 gives a brief comparison between the two.

Table 2.1 Comparison between Industrial Age and E-Age

Industrial Age	***E-Age***
An office	A workspace
Quiet	Noisy
Single task	Multitask
Focused	Directed
Lifetime employment	Lifetime learning
Wages	Ownership
Unions	Teams
Culture	Environment
Accuracy	70% solutions
Play on weekends	Play at work
Seniority	Performance
Tangible products	Intangible products
9 to 5	24/7
Office buildings	Anywhere, anytime
Knowledge is power	Knowledge sharing
Competitors	Networked alliances

Source: Annunzio, S. (2001). e-Leadership – Proven Techniques for Creating an Environment of Speed and Flexibility in the Digital Economy, Simon and Schuster, NY.

This comparison shows a vast gap between the business organizations' behaviors with time. This drastic change has given new meanings to the old fundamentals, one of them being the leadership, which we are going to analyze with an 'e' perspective.

Leadership can be viewed as a dynamic, robust system embedded within larger organizational system. Organizations create structures that define the relationship expected among people who work in those organizations. For example, a hierarchical organizational structure defines, in specific terms that who should be reporting to whom, the boundaries of accountabilities and discretion, and how decisions are to be made. The leadership system in hierarchical organizations builds on the structure by enhancing the relationships that exist between leaders and followers. How? Leadership can be directives, in which case it takes the procedures and rules that go along with the hierarchical structure and makes sure they are properly and fairly administered. Leadership can also be participated within hierarchical structures offering opportunities for people to dialogue about directives and to be more involved in decision-making than the structure itself makes possible. Of course, the leadership system can drag down the organization if it creates inconsistencies, mistrust, and loss of energy, doesn't provide clear direction, and shows a lack of concern for employees.

The global economy is undergoing a major transition with the advancements in the Information Technology. The rapid advances in information and communication technology which allow people to more easily generate, organize, and access information have real implications for the capacities that leaders need. New technology has the potential to affect the distribution of power and the development of relationships in organizations. Therefore, an Information Technology enabled economy is creating a new context for leadership and it becomes important to consider how Information Technology interacts with leadership to influence both the structure and effects of leadership and how leadership, in turn, might influence the adoption of advanced Information Technology and effects on organization.

Leaders in today's business world need to tackle with two interrelated forces. First, the work of organizations and leadership has become increasingly global. An organization's divisions and subunits, customers, stakeholders, and suppliers can often extend worldwide. Second, the exponential explosion in communicating technology has resulted to greater frequency of daily interactions with colleagues, coworkers, subordinates and bosses who are dispersed in different geographic locations. Today, business leaders typically lead teams in which members are located, not in the same office or building, but in different places around the world. Many leaders and team members stay in contact with each other by interacting through telephone, overnight express mail, fax-machine and groupware tools such as e-mail, bulletin boards, chat and video conferencing. In response to these changes people have begun to talk about e-leadership to refer to leaders who conduct many of the processes of leadership largely through electronic channels.

Leadership in the electronic age is surely different. As the impressive and seemingly constant parade of developments in computer and communications technology continues to change our world, we ask what remains the same and what has changed. One tremendously important context for leadership is impact of e-factor on leadership.

It is different because it alters the pattern of how information is acquired, stored, interpreted and disseminated and that, in turn, alters how people are influenced and how decisions are made in organizations. Avolio and Kahai (2003) have pointed that the changes brought about by information technology have altered leadership and its bases of power in a big way. They argued that with the induction of Information Technology in work organizations:

- Access to Information and Media has changed: Followers can now access the same information that leaders had exclusive access to in the past, often before the leaders. This has put pressure on leaders to be prepared to justify their decisions more quickly. Furthermore, there are so many channels through which information flows today that leaders can no longer control releasing the most important information. While releasing information, leaders need to be prepared in the event that it has already been disseminated before.
- Greater workforce Inter connectedness: The interconnectedness of world in today's scenario offers a tremendous opportunity for organizations as they seek ways to respond to rapid shifts in customer demands and increasing globalization of markets. Organizations often respond by linking people across different time zones, cultures, and even competing organizations to complete projects or to provide support within very short time periods. In such organizations an employee can pose a question to a global workforce and expect attention 24 hours/7days.
- It is easier to Reach and Touch others: With the touch of a button the CEO of an organization can have contact with every employee working around the world. He uses email as a conduit for dialogue, sharing of information, projecting his vision of the organization and simply to say "Thank you". There are also times when he unknowingly uses analogies that don't resonate very well in other cultures and might even be perceived as in a different manner.
- Communication is more Indelible than before: Drawn by the convenience of e-mail, a leader may

memorialize remarks that he or she would normally make only in a hushed conversation behind closed doors, by sending them over e-mail to others. Such e-mails can prove to be damaging for the leader and the organization when they are inadvertently exposed, as in a legal investigation.

In the light of above rationalization e-leadership can be well defined as:

"A social influence process mediated by information tech-nology to produce a change in attitudes, feelings, thinking, behaviour, and/or performance with individuals, groups, and/or organizations." (Avolio, Kahai, and Dodge, 2001).

The difference between leadership and e-leadership is highlighted by the fact that in the latter case, not only the work is mediated by information technology, but the collection and dissemination of information required to support organizational work also takes place via information technology. The critical differences may be in 'feeling' the leader's presence, as well as reach, speed, permanence, and perception of a leader's communication. Further, the purpose of e-leadership too is to take the relationship among organizational members defined by an organization's structure.

Thus, it can be concluded that e-leadership ultimately is not about connecting technology, but about connecting people.

CEO of yesmail.com, Dave Tolmie, a permission email marketer, says "The success of a new economy company is based on the collective capabilities of its people. Every company needs to be more collegial and less structured so that the collective talents have a way to manifest themselves."

Microsoft chairman Bill Gates echoed the significance of the work environment in his book 'Business at the Speed of Thought': "The most important 'speed' issue is often not technical but cultural. It's convincing everyone that the company's survival depends on everyone moving as fast as possible."

According to International e-Business consultant Eric Marcus, technology represents only 5 percent of the transformation process. The other 95 percent of a company's metamorphosis is represented by the changes in organizational behavior and culture that are at the heart of e-leadership. As a leader, it's not your job to worry about how your technology is set up. There are people more techno-savvy than you to make those decisions. Your job is more challenging, and ultimately, more significant; to create an environment where everyone can be allowed to come up with their creativity. Technology is merely an enabler in the search for new products and services not an end in itself (Annunzio, S. (2001).

2.2.2 What does E-Leadership Demand?

Susan Annunzio (2001) explains e-leadership in a new style of business management designed specifically to guide top executives as they retool their business to compete in the e-World. According to her–

- e-leadership demands shaking up the corporate culture and fostering an attitude of speed and flexibility in order to facilitate the internal transformation to an environment for the new economy.
- e-leadership demands finding new ways to be a leader: new ways to motivate when you don't see every employee everyday, new ways to communicate your vision and create a culture, and new ways to think about what a company is and what it should look like.
- e-leadership demands managing the clash between baby boomers and the new, brash Generation X and Y workers and finding a way to combine the talents of both groups to achieve success.
- e-leadership demands making the tough decisions that will set a company on the path to success in

the new economy and in the process save jobs, companies, and even entire industries.

- e-leadership demands heroic behavior. It requires abandoning past business models and challenging current assumptions and beliefs. It entails breaking many of the rules we've played by for generations. It means sacrificing the comfort of the status quo in the quest for a new direction that will survive the e-Revolution.
- e-leadership means challenging the accepted belief that running a successful business includes bringing the entire staff under one roof from nine to five everyday. It may require trusting employees to work independently in scattered offices. It may force you to give up some of the symbols of the industrial age; hierarchical organizations, clear lines of authority – even office buildings.
- e-leadership may force you to measure success differently, both corporately and personally. In the future, the world is going to measure success in terms of how many new ideas your company has generated and what kind of talent you're keeping and attracting. Meanwhile, you may need to reconsider golden parachutes, country-club memberships and corner offices – things that were the measures of success in the past. In the world we grew up in, these were ways of saying, "I made it." But they have become increasingly irrelevant.

Amir Hartman states it in his book 'Net Ready'-- "We live in a world of new technology. We are bombarded by it every day. The availability of new tools has affected every company; it's forced them to reevaluate their businesses and rethink their strategies on marketing, distribution, communications, and organizational structure. Even if the strategy ultimately is to have no e-strategy, every business leader has had to rethink his company's place in the world. The new world is about "ruthless execution."

You must have a vision for your company. You need to create an environment where ideas flourish and can be challenged. You need to deal with employees expediently and fairly. You need to communicate and inspire your workforce.

Creating an environment for the new economy is not just a matter of getting up and telling your workforce that you want and need new behavior. It has to be more than symbolic gestures. (Annunzio, 2001)

"If you open up 'new' old companies, you'll see they look a lot like the 'old' old companies,' says Carl Russo, the entrepreneur whose Cerent Corp. became part of Cisco Systems in 1999. "The dress code has changed, which is really neat. But I am not sure that it has anything to do with the core value set the company uses day to day. I thinks it's hard to cut at the core of that."

Here lies your challenge. e-leadership requires creating a workplace where new behavior is encouraged. It demands a new, irreverent way of communicating with employees. You must make sure this behavior isn't merely talked about, but really happens. So, we can say that e-leadership forces you to take the rhetoric of change and put it on the floor.

Indeed, given the rapidity of technology growth in organization and their global reach, it seems that in the near future, e-leadership will be the routine rather than the exception in our thinking about what constitutes organizational leadership.

But the question arises what are the implications for leaders and followers in teams and organizations where interactions are now mediated by information technology? How should we develop leaders to work in this new environment? How does the technology affect trust, motivation, commitment and performance levels? What does "having a presence," mean when the leader is projected into the work group via technology? And what will organizations look like when we move through this time period and fully implement e-leadership, teams and organizations?

As is true that we are using and investing in advanced information technology to lead and to follow with an anticipation of increased profits, Is improved efficiency with enhanced productivity without necessarily knowing the full extent of its impact on human dynamics in organizations really working?

Likewise there are many issues, which are needed to be explored as e-leadership is in its infancy stage. A whole new area is open for the research.

The opportunity for e-leadership exists at the juncture of several powerful forces (Annunzio, 2001):

1. The business world's need for leaders to guide the transformation to the new economy.
2. The speed of the changes in the business climate.
3. The long term economic peril many companies and industries face.
4. The increasing reliance on intellectual capital.
5. The personal motivation among current business leaders to leave a legacy and make a difference in the world.

Prompted by technology, we are experiencing a fundamental reshaping of business, markets and competition. In a survey by Nextera, 97% of business leaders said the rate of change affecting their companies is higher than it was just two years ago. Three-fourth of the respondents said that the rate of change had doubled in a decade.

The road to e-leadership is not an easy one. And perhaps the biggest challenge is learning to be comfortable in the new, less structured, less formal environment where you personally might not be comfortable at all.

2.2.3 Concluding E-Leadership

The global economy is undergoing a major transition that is fundamentally changing how organizations build new markets and relate to their stakeholders. At the center of this transformation is Advanced Information Technology (AIT), which is enabling completely new ways of working and creating value in both the physical world and the virtual world (Rayport and Sviokla, 1995). These changes require a significant adaptation on the part of the leadership in organizations to the new emerging realities of the marketplace, while also continuing to evolve and remain productive in the "old world order". Past leadership research has not focused on issues confronting the leadership in organizations where work is mediated by AIT and it is perhaps too early to identify any empirically based, systematic, patterned variations or to draw any broad conclusions about e-leadership (Avolio, Bruce and Kahai, 1999).

Orlikowski et al. (1995) described the recursive relationship between AIT and the context in which it is used in their work on "technology-use mediation," which they define as a deliberate organizationally sanctioned intervention to help adapt new technology within context and to modify the context to accommodate technology use. They view the introduction and use of new technology as affecting institutions, including the leadership systems that run them, just as institutions can affect the use and adaptation of technology.

An AIT-enabled economy is creating a new context for leadership. Key characteristics of an AIT-enabled economy are real-time information availability, greater knowledge sharing with stakeholders, and the use of this information and knowledge to build "customized" relationships. These customized relationships are putting pressure on organizations and their leaders to be more responsive to their stakeholders. Accompanying these dramatic changes is the global nature of organizational relationships fueled by the ease with which information exchange is enabled across national borders (Drucker, 1993).

Not only are leaders' knowledge structures changing as a result of greater accessibility of information, but the nature of leadership is also changing (Shamir, 1997).

Members of virtual teams have to communicate via AIT, which enables asynchronous, synchronous, one-to-one, or one-to-many communication. Leaders of virtual teams may display "tele-leadership" when they communicate with other team members over electronic media (Shamir and Ben-Ari, 1999). Moreover, leadership may be shared by virtual team members interacting with each other (Shamir, 1997).

AIT and social systems in which AIT are developed and used, influence each other reciprocally (e.g., Klein and Hirschheim, 1983; Orlikowski, 1992; Orlikowski, Yates, Okamura, and Fujimoto, 1995; Weick, 1990; Yates, Orlikowski, and Okamura, 1999).

Similar to the characterization of technology, the leadership system in an organization can be characterized by its spirit or intent. For instance, the spirit of a participative leadership system is to increase involvement of organizational members in decision-making by fostering openness in communication and collaboration among organizational members. Consistency between the leadership's spirit and AIT's spirit is important for faithful appropriations, and will likely predict how successful or unsuccessful insertion of new technology will be in an organization. (Avolio, Bruce J. and Surinder Kahai, 2001).

Some of the studies suggest that an electronic interface is not a substitute for face-to-face communication (Abel, 1990; Sproull and Kiesler, 1991). Studies further suggest that trust is temporal and fragile for groups with no face-to-face communication, which are culturally divided, or have no common past or plans for future collaboration, making CMC tools less effective (Jarvenpaa and Leidner, 1998; Jones and George, 1998; Meyerson et al., 1996).

The use of ICT such as video and audio for building trust is considered to represent slower progress towards full cooperation and is vulnerable to opportunistic behavior (Das and Teng, 1998)

According to Niederman and Beise (1996), face-to-face communication was found to be more effective than audio conferencing for tasks which rely on interpersonal communication and are more complex in nature.

Research has also shown that the dispersion and dislocation characterizing virtual organizations may reduce communication among employees, increase their feelings of isolation, and consequently reduce their commitment to the organization (Huff, C., L. Sproull, and S. Kiesler, 1989)

Staples (1997) reported that organizational commitment of their employees was one of the most important abiding concerns of managers of virtual workers.

Research of social psychologists have previously shown that computer-mediated intra-group communication is unable to support the fuller range of communicative acts typically employed by face-to-face groups (McKinlay, A., Procter, R., and Dunnet,1999, Spears, R., Lea, M. and Lee, S., 1990).

O' Connell's (1998) assessment of the impact of IT on human relationships and the system of interactions within the organization is worth mentioning. He contends that with the induction of Information Technology in work organizations:

- Opportunities for face-to-face contact will be diminished and information from non-verbal cues will be reduced. Consequently, opportunities for random, spontaneous information sharing will be reduced. Managers will need to structure work relationships to provide more opportunities for face-to-face contact to occur. Meanings will be derived increasingly from texts and symbols.

- More informal messages and "short-circuiting" of the hierarchy will occur as new formats are accepted due to the remote nature of an electronic network. Organization structure and formal information will be redefined.
- Channel effects will mean that messages of affect and value will decrease. Digitized data, with less context and interpretation, will be the norm. Consequently, decision-making may be impaired rather than enhanced. Ambiguity in interpreting information will increase and the quality of decision could decrease with the lack of organizational values and context. Organizations will need to work harder at communicating their values and corporate history. Managers will have to seek new ways of communicating the affective components of messages. New and improved decision-making skills will be needed.
- Trust will play a changed role in new environment. Trust develops with shared experience, values, and give-and-take that are the result of human communication. Satellites, electronic mail, and networks could reduce the dimensions of trust to which we are accustomed. New dimensions of trust may spring up in their place.
- The computer imposes a discipline of linear thinking. Data is processed at speed that increases with each new version of the chip. Consequently, people may become less patient and tolerant for individual styles of communicating. Organizations may find themselves becoming less tolerant of people who do not think or perceive in a strict, linear mode. Organizations will need to find ways to encourage and protect non-linear thinking and communicating.

- Expectations of work performance may be machine driven. As we become accustomed to the speed and accuracy of the computer, we may expect employees to have the same qualities and produce in similar manner. Employees in some organizations will perceive this as dehumanizing and not congenial. Unions will take up the human environment as an issue. New ways of defining and using performance standards will be needed.

2.3 Present Study

Leadership is shared and distributed in organizations. Individuals at different levels and in different positions perform leadership roles. The key tasks for leaders, from the top management team to front line managers, are to ensure that the right choices are made about the organization's objectives and strategies; that employees are motivated to pursue these objectives and strategies; that the organizational structure, culture and design of roles and responsibilities enables individuals and groups to achieve these objectives; and that employees are sufficiently supported, skilled and confident to be effective. Effective leadership is critical for promoting individual, group and organizational performance.

There are two main types of leaders in organizations: top management leaders who take more of the responsibility for setting the strategic direction for the organization, and leaders who have line management and staff supervision responsibilities. The leadership role performed by line managers has the potential to influence individual and group performance. These leaders have a critical role to play:

- Clarifying individual and group objectives and ensuring that these contribute to achieving the organization's goals.
- Defining work design and structures that enable individuals and groups to be effective.

- Ensuring that individuals and groups have the resources and support they need.

In addition, these leaders have relevant task expertise, abilities and attitudes that through monitoring, feedback and coaching will help individuals and groups to successfully achieve their tasks.

In the light of the theories and concepts presented in the previous and current chapter, it has been found that studies conducted in past in the area of leadership have not talked about the state of affairs where work is mediated by information technology. It is too intricate to identify or infer any conclusion about e-leadership. Past literature shows that most of the efforts have been made to study virtual teams where team members are geographically dispersed.

As a result, it was really hard to find even a comprehensive definition of e-leadership. E-leadership has been viewed in different ways by different researchers. Research in the area of e-leadership is in its infancy stage. No conclusions can be drawn from the available literature about e-leadership.

In the present study an attempt has been made to study e-leadership in business organizations in Indian context. The idea was to do a comparative analysis i.e., Traditional Leadership vis-à-vis E-Leadership: A Comparative Analysis of Business Organizations.

2.3.1 Operational Definition of Traditional Leadership and E-Leadership

In the current study traditional leadership or simply leadership has been considered as "a way where leader is physically present with his team members and leader-follower interaction is face-to-face irrespective of the type of leadership followed by the leader."

E-leadership has been viewed from a perspective "where leader is not physically present with the team members and interacts with them through ways which are IT mediated. He has been called as an e-leader."

2.3.2 Components of the Study

The researcher has made an attempt to find out the impact of physical absence of the leader with respect to some of the dimensions associated with leadership and chosen for the study. The variables chosen for the study are Trust, Commitment, Organizational Culture, Performance and Motivation.

Figures 2.3 and 2.4 present a diagrammatic representation of the scheme of the study.

2.3.3 Schematic Representation of the Framework Proposed for the Study

The models represent that the various variables chosen for the study are influenced by the phenomenon of leadership and e-leadership.

It has been assumed that e-leadership, has much more impact on all the variables chosen for the study i.e., Trust, Commitment, Organizational Culture, Performance and Motivation as compared to the traditional leadership as depicted in Figure 2.3.

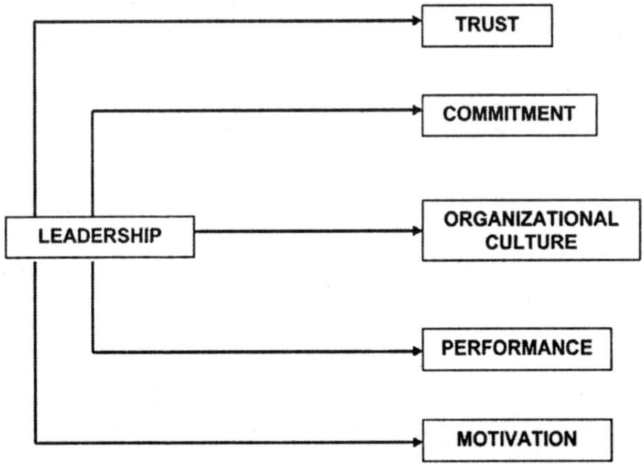

Figure 2.3 Schematic Representation for Leadership

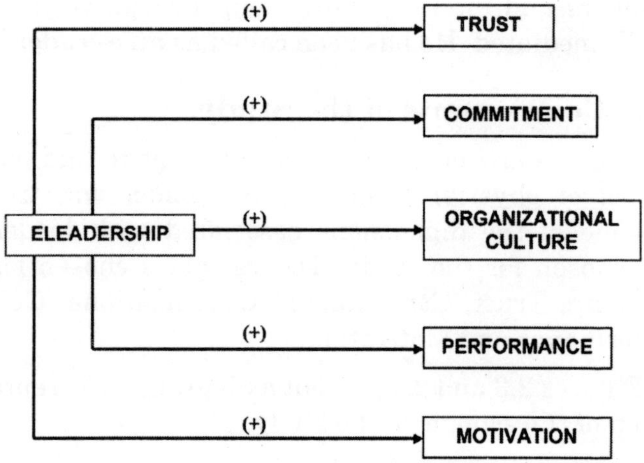

Figure 2.4 Schematic Representation for E-leadership

3 REVIEW OF LITERATURE

Review of Literature

In today's business world, effective leadership is gaining precedence over effective management. If effective management principles alone were once considered as the essentials of organizational and business success, today the success of organizations and businesses are equally or perhaps more dependent on effective and futuristic leadership. With the information and communication revolution of the late 1990s, many glorious business corporations of the past have been doomed to failure, the reason often being attributed as the failure of the leadership to lead and steer the organization through the fast paced changes in the business scenario brought about by the revolution.

This chapter presents a review of literature of the major dimensions chosen for the study under leadership/e-leadership and contributes to the success of present day leaders and business organizations.

3.1 Motivation

3.1.1 Motivation as A Concept

The term 'motivation' is derived from the Latin word

'movere' which means "to move". It is an inner state that causes people to behave in certain ways. The common frame of reference includes one or the following words in the definition of motivation: drives, goals, incentives, desires, wants, need as almost every body has their own definition of motivation.

Motivation can be referred as a catalyst as it determines the intensity of willingness and the level of efforts a person put for the achievement of organizational objectives.

Some of the definitions of motivation given by eminent scholars are:

According to Robert Dubin (1970),

"Motivation is the complex set of forces starting and keeping a person at work in an organization. Motivation is something that moves the person to action, and continues him in the course of action already initiated."

Dalton E. McFarland (1974) stated that:

"Motivation refers to the way in which urges, drives, desires, aspirations, and strivings or needs direct, control or explain the behaviour of human beings."

In the words of C.B Mamoria (1995),

"Motivation is a willingness to expend energy to achieve a goal or reward. It is a force that activates dormant energies and sets in motion the action of the people. It is the function that kindles a burning passion for action among the human beings of an organization."

According to Kreitner (1995), motivation has been defined as:

"The psychological process that gives behavior purpose and direction."

Buford, Bedeian, and Lindner (1995) states that:

"Motivation is a predisposition to behave in a purposive manner to achieve specific, unmet needs."

3.1.2 Theories of Motivation

Despite the fact that motivation is a basic psychological process, much relevant motivation theories have been identified so far. Over time, these major theoretical streams of research in motivation were classified into two major schools: the content theories of motivation and the process theories of motivation. A classification of these theories can be depicted from the figure 3.1 as given below.

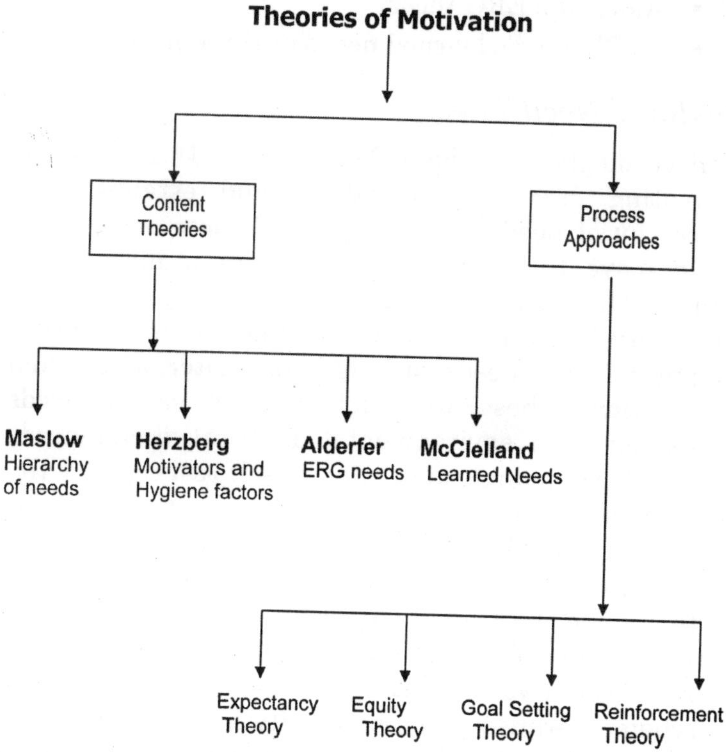

Figure 3.1: Classification of Major Motivation Theories

Content Theories

Content (or need) theories of motivation focus on factors internal to the individual that energize and direct behavior. In general, such theories regard motivation as the product of internal drives that compel an individual to act or move (hence, "motivate") toward the satisfaction of individual needs. The content theories of motivation are based in large part on early theories of motivation that traced the paths of action backward to their perceived origin in internal drives. Major content theories of motivation are:

- Maslow's hierarchy of needs
- Herzberg's motivator-hygiene theory
- Alderfer's ERG theory
- McClelland's learned needs or three-need theory

Maslow's Need Theory

Psychologist Abraham Maslow (1954) focused on motivating forces in individuals and established a "hierarchy of needs." According to Maslow, individuals would move to satisfy their needs in a hierarchical manner. Once a need is satisfied, it no longer has have the ability to motivate. At the bottom of the hierarchy are physiological needs such as food, shelter, and sexual gratification. These were followed by safety needs (protection from environmental dangers), social needs (love and belonging), and esteem (self-respect and the approval of others). The highest need is the need for self-fulfillment, which involves deriving a sense of value and satisfaction from one's work. While people generally fill these needs in order, Maslow recognized that the hierarchy was flexible within individuals, and that priorities could vary. Maslow did not include money in his schema because of the ambiguity in the meaning of money. For some people, money is a way to achieve the basic requirements of food and shelter. Others view money as a measure to satisfy their need for self-fulfillment.

Herzberg's Theory

Herzberg, Mausner, and Snyderman (1959) interviewed 200 engineers and accountants to explore what factors were motivating. They concluded that many factors that were thought to be motivating, such as pay and managerial style, were not motivating at all. Herzberg (1966) proposed that job satisfaction and dissatisfaction are not opposite ends of a continuum, but rather represent two distinct variables. Intrinsic motivational factors (called "satisfiers") included achievement, recognition, and responsibility. Extrinsic factors (called "hygiene factors") consisted of things like pay, status, job security, and management style. Herzberg theorized that lack of satisfiers would not cause dissatisfaction. The presence of hygiene factors would not cause satisfaction, but their absence would cause dissatisfaction.

Herzberg developed a list of factors that are based on Maslow's hierarchy of needs, except that his version is more closely related to the working environment.

Herzberg's Hygiene and Motivational Factors

Hygiene or Dissatisfiers:

- Working conditions
- Policies and administrative practices
- Salary and Benefits
- Supervision
- Status
- Job security
- Co-workers
- Personal life

Motivators or Satisfiers:

- Recognition
- Achievement
- Advancement
- Growth
- Responsibility
- Job challenge

Hygiene factors must be present in the job before motivators can be used to stimulate that person. That is, one cannot use motivators until all the hygiene factors are met. Herzberg's needs are specifically job related and reflect some of the distinct things that people want from their work as opposed to Maslow's Hierarchy of Needs which reflect all the needs in a person's life.

While Hertzberg's two-factor theory generated considerable research, "repeated factor analytic studies of job attitudes have failed to demonstrate the existence of two independent factors corresponding to motivators and hygienes" (Campbell, 1970).

Alderfer's ERG Theory

The ERG theory is an extension of Maslow's hierarchy of needs. Alderfer identified three categories of needs. Alderfer suggested that needs could be classified into three categories, rather than five. These three types of needs are existence, relatedness, and growth.

Existence needs are the desires for material and physical well being. These needs are satisfied with food, water, air, shelter, working conditions, pay, and fringe benefits.

Relatedness needs are the desires to establish and maintain interpersonal relationships. These needs are satisfied with relationships with family, friends, supervisors, subordinates, and co-workers.

Growth needs are the desires to be creative, to make useful and productive contributions, and to have opportunities for personal development.

The ERG theory differs from the hierarchy of needs in that it does not suggest that lower-level needs must be completely satisfied before upper-level needs become motivational. ERG theory also suggests that if an individual is continually unable to meet upper-level needs then the person will regress and lower-level needs will become the major determinant of his motivation.

McClelland's Learned Needs Theory

McClelland's theory suggests that individuals learn needs from their culture. Three of the primary needs in this theory are the need for affiliation (n Aff), the need for power (n Pow), and the need for achievement (n Ach).

Achievement motivated people thrive on pursuing and attaining goals. They like to be able to control the situations in which they are involved. They take moderate risks. They like to get immediate feedback on how they have done. They tend to be preoccupied with a task-orientation towards the job to be done.

Power motivated individuals see almost every situation as an opportunity to seize control or dominate others. They love to influence others. They like to change situations whether or not it is needed. They are willing to assert themselves when a decision needs to be made.

Affiliation motivated people are usually friendly and like to socialize with others. This may distract them from their performance requirements. They will usually respond to an appeal for cooperation.

The main point of the learned needs theory is that when one of these needs is strong in a person, it has the potential to motivate behavior that leads to its satisfaction.

Process Theories

Process (or cognitive) theories of motivation focus on conscious human decision processes as an explanation of motivation. The process theories are concerned with determining how individual behavior is energized, directed, and maintained in the specifically willed and self-directed human cognitive processes. Process theories of motivation are based on early cognitive theories which posit that behavior is the result of conscious decision-making processes. The major process theories of motivation are:

- Expectancy Theory
- Equity Theory
- Goal-setting theory
- Reinforcement theory.

Expectancy Theory

Vroom's Expectancy theory states that an individual will act in a certain way based on the expectation that the act will be followed by a given outcome and on the attractiveness of that outcome to the individual. This motivational model (Vroom, 1964) has been modified by several people, to include Porter and Lawler (Porter et. al., 1968). Vroom's Expectancy Theory is written as a formula:

Valence × Expectancy × Instrumentality = Motivation

- **Valence (Reward)** = the amount of desire for a goal (What is the reward?)
- **Expectancy (Performance)** = the strength of belief that work related effort will result in the completion of the task (How hard will I have to work to reach the goal?)
- **Instrumentality (Belief)** = the belief that the reward will be received once the task is completed (Will they notice the effort I put forth?)

The product of valence, expectancy, and instrumentality is motivation. It can be thought of as the strength of the drive towards a goal. For example, if an employee wants to move up through the ranks, then promotion has a high valence for that employee. If the employee believes that high performance will result in good reviews, then the employee has a high expectancy. However, if the employee believes the company will not promote from within, then the employee has low instrumentality, and the employee will not be motivated to perform better.

Equity Theory

Equity theory says that it is not the actual reward that motivates, but the perception, and the perception is based not on the reward in isolation, but in comparison with the efforts that went into getting it and the rewards and efforts of others. If everyone got a 5% raise, B is likely to feel quite pleased with her raise, even if she worked harder than everyone else. But if A got an even higher raise, B perceives that she worked just as hard as A, she will be unhappy.

In other words, people's motivation results from a ratio of ratios: a person compares the ratio of reward to effort with the comparable ratio of reward to effort that they think others are getting.

Of course, in terms of actually predicting how a person will react to a given motivator, this will get pretty complicated:

1. People do not have complete information about how others are rewarded. So they are going on perceptions, rumors, and inferences.
2. Some people are more sensitive to equity issues than others.
3. Some people are willing to ignore short-term inequities as long as they expect things to work out in the long-term.

Goal-Setting Theory

The goal-setting theory posits that goals are the most important factors affecting the motivation and behavior of employees. This motivation theory was developed primarily by Edwin Locke and Gary Latham (1990). Goal-setting theory emphasizes the importance of specific and challenging goals in achieving motivated behavior. Specific goals often involve quantitative targets for improvement in a behavior of interest. Research indicates that specific performance goals are much more effective than those in which a person is told to "do your best." Challenging goals are difficult but not impossible to attain. Empirical research supports the proposition that goals that are both specific and challenging are more motivational than vague goals or goals that are relatively easy to achieve.

Several factors may moderate the relationship between specific and challenging goals and high levels of motivation. The first of these factors is goal commitment, which simply means that the more dedicated the individual is to achieving the goal, the more they will be motivated to exert effort toward goal accomplishment. Some researches suggest that having employees participate in goal setting will increase their level of goal commitment. A second factor relevant to goal-setting theory is self-efficacy, which is the individual's belief that he or she can successfully complete a particular task. If individuals have a high degree of self-efficacy, they are likely to respond more positively to specific and challenging goals than if they have a low degree of self-efficacy.

Reinforcement Theory

The reinforcement theory of motivation (also called contin-gency theory) is an outgrowth of the behaviorist school of psychology. Skinner (1974) is the most well-known proponent of the theory. The basic principles of the theory are: (1) reinforced behavior tends to be repeated, (2) reward is more effective than punishment, (3) feedback is necessary for improvement (4) rewards should be given without delay, and (5) rewards should be given for successive approximations of the desired behavior (Schneier, 1974).

Collins and Porras (1989) believe that motivation is the result of people doing a job that they think is worthwhile.

They assert that motivation is not something that needs to be cultivated directly. Instead, it is a natural outcome of workers who believe in the mission, vision, and purpose of an organization. The "purpose" of an organization is a set of broad, enduring, inspirational, and fundamental reasons for the existence of the organization. The purpose provides a clear sense of direction by stating what members of the organization want to contribute to the world. The "mission" is a clearly defined and achievable goal. It provides a focal point of motivation. The "vision" is usually defined as being able to foresee the future and developing a plan to meet the future needs. Collins and Porras (1989) define vision as "the ability to see the potential in or necessity of opportunities right in front of you. . . vision isn't forecasting the future, it is creating the future by taking action in the present."

3.1.3 Motivation and Leadership/E-Leadership

Motivation and Leadership are, arguably, the two fundamental areas that organizational researchers and practicing managers look to in order to understand behaviour inside organizations.

Since the scientific investigation of motivation and leadership began, in the early 1900s, motivation and leadership have received such considerable and sustained attention because most perspectives on these subjects have assumed that they involve principal behavioural factors that are specially critical to the functioning of contemporary organizations. Managers and researchers can not avoid a concern with the behavioural requirements of an organization.

In addition to deploying financial and physical resources, every organization must utilize its human resources effectively.

Scientific developments in the areas of motivation and leadership proceeded essentially independently of one another for several decades. Early approaches to motivation such as instinct theories, emerged around the turn of the century. The scientific investigation of leadership commenced somewhat later, with trait theories being popular in the 1930s. From these two beginning points, progress in the study of motivation and leadership was made for many years with very little interaction between the two topic areas.

Researchers in the area of leadership generally did not acknowledge a role for motivation in their theories until relatively recently. That is, early trait, behaviour, and contingency theories of leadership did not use ideas from the area of motivation to identify relevant independent variables (i.e., traits, behaviours, or situation contingencies) or to explain the intervening process between these independent variables and the dependent variables of interest (e.g., group effectiveness). Recently, however, leadership researchers, particularly those studying charismatic and transformational approaches have stated to draw more heavily on motivational concepts in an effort to understand certain organizational phenomena.

A major impetus driving organizational researchers and practicing managers to emphasize both motivation and leadership comes from recent developments in contemporary organizations. Organizations function within, and depend upon their environments. However, by every measure, the environments of most organizations are becoming more turbulent. The globalization of the world's markets, the dizzying pace of advances in Information Technologies, the impact of government regulations, and the growing sophistication of the world's capital markets have all been cited as reasons for the relentless escalation in the rate of environmental change and in the competitive intensity experienced by most organizations (e.g., Kanter, 1989; Kotter, 1988; Pfeffer, 1994). Under these circumstances, many of the structural features that are intended to guide behaviour inside organizations quickly become ill suited to shifting conditions.

As organizations attempt to adapt to increasing environmental volatility and competitive intensity, organizational effectiveness, or even survival, may depend on management's ability to energize and direct organizational employees to apply intense and sustained effort toward the goals of the organization, even when these goals may be subject to frequent modifications. Couched in this way, the importance of, and the connections between the topics of motivation and leadership in an organizational context are apparent. Therefore, researchers and managers must draw on both topics to understand and then effectively influence behaviour in today's organizations.

The link between motivation and leadership can be illustrated by their interaction with an overwhelming force, which is affecting almost all organizations as the 21st century begins i.e. advanced technology. Such technology, in one form or another, is crucial to the effective functioning of virtually every organization; yet it is insufficient by itself for guaranteeing the highest level of performance. While technology provides a base for superior performance, it is inevitably up to the human resources to use that technology to its highest potential in order to help organizations attain their most for reaching and challenging goals and objectives. Here is where motivation and leadership intersect. Without both high levels of motivated work behaviour and exceptional leadership, an organization's technological capabilities are likely to remain underutilized and less-than optimally applied.

Another example of a place where a joint consideration of motivation and leadership can help illuminate issues is the increasingly important topic of teams in organizations. Many contemporary organizations are attempting to develop a more team-oriented culture in order to maximize the efforts and initiatives of small groups of people. How leadership is distributed and displayed within such groups has a lot to do with whether a team like feeling is generated among the members, and this, in turn, is assumed to affect the resulting motivation of those group members. We can probably all think of organizational groups we have known where leadership appears to be missing and member motivation is essentially absent or at least quite low. Likewise, it is not too difficult for most of us to point to groups we have observed- certain collegiate or professional sports teams are obvious examples that exhibit exactly the opposite pattern: a combination of strong leadership and motivation. When the subject is teams and teamwork, leadership and motivation seem inseparably linked.

Although these two concepts are interrelated, it is also important to point out that they are not totally intertwined and overlapping. These are certainly aspects of motivation that are strongly affected by variables other than leadership and there are many consequences of leadership beyond its effect on motivation. Nevertheless, the degree of fundamental connection between the two areas has been growing in recent years, particularly as more comprehensive analyses of organizational behaviour have developed and as new organizational issues have arisen. For instance, in the past decade or so there has been considerable interest focused on such topics as high involvement management, self-management, transformational leadership, charismatic leadership and learning organizations.

Mintzberg (1973) described the role of a leader as being the person responsible for the motivation and activation of subordinates.

A stream of leadership research (e.g., Blades, 1986; Fiedler and Garcia, 1987) considers how the resources available to a leader such as his ability and leadership style, relate to group performance under varying conditions of group member motivation, cohesion, and ability.

Conceptualization of transformational leadership by Bass (1985) seems to be directly involved with enhancing follower motivation.

Building on the work of Burns (1978), Bass (1985) defined transformational leadership and established a measurement instrument for the construct. From his perspective, transformational leaders motivate their followers to perform beyond normal expectations by transforming their thoughts and attitudes. They enlist their followers to buy into their vision and strive for its fulfillment. To accomplish this, transformational leaders exhibit the following kinds of behaviors: attributed charisma, inspirational motivation, intellectual stimulation, and individualized consideration (Bass and Avolio, 1994; Conger 1999).

Also studying transactional leadership, Hunt (1991) found that this type of leadership motivates followers by appealing to their self-interests (pay, status, rewards) because these are used in exchange for work.

3.2 Trust

3.2.1 Trust as a Concept

Trust in sociology is a relationship between people. It involves the suspension of disbelief that one person will have towards another person or idea. It especially involves having one person thinking that the other person or idea is benevolent, competent/good, or honest/true.

A common feature shared by all social-psychological theories and studies is that they conceive trust as only a psychological state at the individual level. In a recent review of the literature, Kramer (1999) notes differences among various theories, but states that 'despite divergence in such particulars, most trust theories agree that, whatever else its essential features, trust is fundamentally a psychological state.' Trust has been viewed by these theories primarily as an interpersonal phenomenon. Trust building and erosion have been attributed to cognitive and affective processes that occur at the individual level, stemming from the characteristics and behaviours of the trustee. Because it is so central to human relationships, many definitions of trust have been offered.

Based on a cross-disciplinary review of trust studies, Rousseau et al. (1998) offered the following consensus definition:

"Trust is a psychological state comprising the intention to accept vulnerability based upon positive expectations of the intentions or behavior of another."

Moorman, Zaltman, and Deshpande (1992) stated that:

"Trust is defined as a willingness to rely on an exchange partner in whom one has confidence."

According to Mayer et al. (1995):

"Trust is the willingness of a party to be vulnerable to the actions of another party based on the expectation that the other party will perform a particular action important to the trustor, irrespective of the ability to monitor or control that other party."

3.2.2 Forms of Trust

We can study trust in two basic forms viz:

- Personal trust
- Abstract trust

Personal trust is trust in known or close individuals and is based on the expectation that the individual will perform in line with one's legitimate aspirations of the relationship or contract entered into.

Abstract trust, also known as systems trust, is trust in social systems, which include organizations, markets and state systems – it is trust that operates across time and space (Morrison and Firmstone, 2000). According to Luhmann (1979), systems trust or abstract trust is trust that includes reflexivity and a conscious approach to arrangements.

Abstract trust is essential for social solidarity, or social cohesion. Without abstract trust, complex social organization could not exist. Indeed, without abstract trust, modernity as we know it would be impossible. Personal trust allows only for very primitive association, including very restricted commercial exchange (Morrison and Firmstone, 2000). As Luhmann (1979) states: 'without trust only very simple forms of human co-operation which can be transacted on the spot are possible, and even individual action is much too sensitive to disruption to be capable of being planned, without trust, beyond the assured moment'.

Many theories of trust are grounded in social exchange theory (Blau, 1964), which assumes that trust emerges through the repeated exchange of benefits between two individuals. Because it addresses the process of initiating and expanding social exchanges, this theory provides a useful lens for examining the motivational mechanisms underlying the initiation of trustworthy behavior. However, managers and employees are also involved in an economic exchange relationship. Theories of economic exchange like agency theory (Eisenhardt, 1989), place little emphasis on trust, but they do offer explanations for managerial behavior, such as monitoring and control, that are commonplace in organizations and that affect employees' perceptions of trust. They also capture the economic context in which social exchange relationships develop.

3.2.3 Theories of Trust

Agency Theory

Agency theorists describe the structuring of economic exchange relationships between two parties (Eisenhardt, 1989; Jensen and Meckling, 1976; Noorderhaven, 1992). A principal-agent relationship exists when one party (the principal) contracts with another party (the agent) to perform a task involving delegation of decision making in exchange for compensation. Agency theorists examine how principals and agents attempt to structure the relationship to protect their own interests. Applying agency theory to manager-employee dyads, one can consider the employee to be an agent and the manager to represent the interests of the principal.

This perspective assumes self-interest, thereby implying that individuals strive to maximize individual utility and that both parties seek to minimize risks associated with the relationship. Agents bear risk as a function of how they are compensated. To the extent that their compensation is based on outcomes that are beyond their control, the risk to them is greater. In contrast, the principal faces the risk of opportunism and incompetence on the part of agents. The risk of opportunism is greater when the principal lacks information about agents' actions (i.e., information asymmetry) and when competing incentives or goals (i.e., goal incongruence) for agents motivate them to engage in actions other than what was contracted by the principal. For example, when employees are contracted to perform a job that the manager cannot directly observe, the manager faces the risk that the employees may shirk their duty. To minimize agency risk, principals generally either monitor agents' behavior to ensure contract compliance or base agents' compensation on task outcomes to align the agents' goals with the principals'.

Social Exchange Theory

Although the formal or contractual relationship in employment is economically driven, a social element to such relationships typically evolves. Social exchange theory (Blau, 1964) helps to explain the dynamics of such exchanges. In a social exchange, one individual voluntarily provides a benefit to another, invoking an obligation of the other party to reciprocate by providing some benefit in return. Proving oneself trustworthy may be problematic when one is initially forming such social exchange relationships. Blau (1964) argues, however, that trust may be generated through two means: (1) through the regular discharge of obligations (i.e., by reciprocating for benefits received from others) and (2) through the gradual expansion of exchanges over time.

Social exchanges differ from economic ones in several fundamental ways (Blau, 1964). First, social exchanges may involve extrinsic benefits with economic value (e.g., information and advice) or intrinsic benefits without any direct objective economic utility (e.g., social support). Further, extrinsic benefits often are expressions of support and friendship and, thus, have intrinsic value as well. Therefore, exchanges that have little or unclear economic benefit can have a strong impact on the social dimension of a relationship.

Second, whereas benefits in economic exchanges are formal and often contracted explicitly, such benefits are rarely specified a priori or explicitly negotiated in social exchanges. Thus, providing benefits is a voluntary action.

Finally, because such behavior is voluntary, there is no guarantee that benefits will be reciprocated or that reciprocation will result in receipt of future benefits. The exchange of benefits involves uncertainty, particularly in early stages of the relationship, when the risk of nonreciprocation is relatively high. Consequently, relationships evolve slowly, starting with the exchange of relatively low-value benefits and escalating to higher-value benefits as the parties demonstrate their trustworthiness.

Taken together, agency theory and social exchange theory expand the picture of trust formation in organizations. An agency theory lens highlights the formal economic context and selfinterest motive, as well as the behavioral consequences. It also delineates factors that contribute to the risk of opportunism and identifies how the exchange relationship can be structured to minimize this risk. Although implying how relationship context contributes to risk, agency theory takes a relatively static view of relationships.

A social exchange theory lens, however, highlights dynamic elements of the exchange relationship. It emphasizes the exchange process, including its development over time, and indicates that successful social exchanges should influence perceptions of risk of nonreciprocation (i.e., opportunism) and trust. This lens also helps us identify when, under conditions of agency risk, an individual is likely to trust another party, rather than impose greater controls. For example, imagine two managers each working with a subordinate who telecommutes. From an agency theory perspective, information asymmetry is high in both cases and, therefore, agency risk (i.e., risk of opportunism) is high. However, the manager who forms a strong social bond with his or her subordinate through the process of successful social exchanges should perceive less risk of opportunism, despite equal levels of information asymmetry.

In summary, agency theory lens identifies relatively static, contextual factors associated with the risk of opportunism in economic exchanges. It is under these circumstances of agency risk that social exchange theory is particularly relevant, for it helps us examine when one party is willing to trust another rather than impose control on the other. Specifically, social exchange theory lens suggests that by habitually discharging one's obligations, trust develops that may mitigate the risk of opportunism inherent in the organizational context. Therefore, managers may reduce the risk of opportunism by engaging in trustworthy behavior.

3.2.4 Trust and Leadership/E-leadership

Much has been written in recent years about trust in organizational authorities. This attention stems from a general belief that recent trends in the organizational field, such as higher rates of environmental and technological change, greater needs for flexibility and cooperation, increased reliance on teams and teamwork, and changes in employment relationships and career patterns. increase the importance of trust in organizations (Mayer et al. 1995; Rousseau et al. 1998).

The role of trust in business has been drawing increasing attention recently from management researchers and practitioners alike (Hosmer, 1995; Kramer and Tyler, 1996; Mayer, Davis, and Schoorman, 1995). There appears to be a general consensus among researchers that trust is important and useful in a range of organizational activities, such as team work, leadership, goal setting, performance appraisal, development of labor relations, and negotiation (Mayer et al., 1995; Morris and Moberg, 1994).

Scholars have widely acknowledged that trust can lead to cooperative behavior among individuals, groups, and organizations (e.g., Axelrod, 1984; Gambetta, 1988; Good, 1988; Mayer, Davis, and Schoorman, 1995; McAllister, 1995). Today, in an era when organizations are searching for new ways to promote cooperation between people and groups to enhance the value they create, it is not surprising that interest in the concept of trust and, in particular, how to promote or actualize it is increasing (Kramer and Tyler, 1996).

Trust has received a great deal of attention from scholars in the base disciplines of social psychology (e.g., Deutsch, 1960; Lewicki and Bunker, 1995; Lindskold, 1978), sociology (e.g., Lewis and Weigert, 1985; Strub & Priest, 1976), and economics (e.g., Dasgupta, 1988; Williamson, 1991), as well as in more applied areas like management (e.g., Gulati, 1995; Lane and Bachman, 1996) and marketing (e.g., Anderson and Weitz, 1989; Dwyer, Schurr, and Oh, 1987; Moorman, Zaltman, and Deshpande, 1992). Each of these bodies of literature offer unique insights into the nature of trust and the processes through which trust develops.

However, although multidisciplinary interest has added to the richness of the construct, there have been surprisingly few attempts to integrate the various perspectives on trust (Lewicki and Bunker, 1995; Mayer et al., 1995). In one such effort, Shapiro, Sheppard, and Cheraskin (1992) propose that trust has three bases: (1) deterrence-based trust emphasizes costs and benefits, (2) knowledge-based trust requires getting to know the target, and (3) identification-based trust forms on the basis of common values.

Zucker (1986) suggests that trust may be based on (1) the process of exchange, (2) characteristics of the exchange partners, or (3) societal institutions.

Focusing on characteristics of the trustee, Mayer et al. (1995) suggest that a target's ability, benevolence, and integrity are the primary factors leading to trust.

Each model suggests that trustors make assessments about the trustworthiness of targets, and that such assessments may be along multiple dimensions.

Developing an integrated model of trust is particularly difficult, given the vagueness and idiosyncrasies in defining trust across multiple disciplines and orientations (Andaleeb, 1992; Barber, 1983; Mayer et al., 1995; McAllister, 1995). From a related perspective, many writers on leadership view trust as an essential component of leadership (for example, Bennis and Nanus 1985; Locke et al. 1991; Zand 1972).

Some even regard it as a defining component. For instance, Solomon (1996) asserts that "leadership is an emotional relationship of trust".

Conger and Kanungo (1998) state that "leading implies fostering changes in followers through the building of trust and credibility".

Followers' trust in the leader occupies a central role in several theories of leadership, either explicitly or implicitly. For instance, the Leader-Member-Exchange theory (Graen and Uhl-Bien, 1995) focuses on the quality of the dyadic relationships between the leader and group members, and includes trust as a major component of this relationship.

In a similar vein, theories of charismatic leadership by House (1977) and Conger and Kanungo (1998) include a follower's trust in the leader as an essential component of the charismatic relationship.

Several studies have examined the antecedents of subordinates' trust in their managers or leaders. Butler (1991) examined the relationship between 'conditions of trust', which include several characteristics of managers' behaviour, such as consistency and honesty, and the overall trust of subordinates in their superiors. Podsakoff et al. (1990) found that subordinates' trust in their managers mediated the relationship between managers' transformational leadership behaviours and subordinates' organizational citizenship behaviours. Conger and Kanungo (1998) have shown that charismatic leader behaviours increase reverence for the leader, which in turn increases trust in the leader. Trust in leaders was found to be significantly related to transformational leadership (Connell et al., 2002).

3.3 Organizational Culture

3.3.1 Organization Culture as a Concept

In a fundamental sense, a culture exists when people come to share a common frame of reference for interpreting and reacting towards one another and towards the world in which they live. This common frame of reference includes language, values, beliefs and interpretation of experiences. It is reflected in customs, folkways, communication and observable features of the community including rituals, rites, celebrations, legends, myths and heroic saga.

The first step towards understanding the essence of organization's culture is to appreciate that it is a concept rather than a thing. This distinction is crucial. A thing can be discovered and truth established about it, for example, through empirical research. However, a concept is created in people's mind – that is, it must be conjured up, defined and refined. There is no final authoritative source or experiment to settle disagreements about what it is or what comprises it. In organizational studies, theorists have come up with different ways of defining organization culture. Smircich (1983) pointed out, that both fundamentalist and interpretivist scholars have written about and produced studies on organization culture, but she argues that these two groups understand organizational culture in entirely different ways. To a functionalist, a culture is something that an organization has – "a set of characteristics that an organization possesses." The interpretivist sees culture "as the essence of organizational life". It is described according to the meanings and the ways in which the culture itself is enacted or performed through communication.

People get affected by the culture in which they live. Values, beliefs, expected behavior of a family are taught to its members through the process of socialization within the family. The same is true for the organizations. When people join an organization they have certain values and beliefs but they may not be sufficient for achieving organizational goals. Hence, they are required to adapt to the culture of the organization. Every organization has missions and goals and to attain these, it adapts unique modes and methods of operations. In the process of achieving the corporate mission, participants internalize organizational values and norms to give meaningful expressions to the same in their day-to-day activities. Thus all the members of an organization come to adapt shared values, beliefs, norms, attitudes, ways of doing things and practices which are unique to the organization. This is called the culture of the organization. As Hagberg & Heifetz (1998) concede that:

"Culture drives the organization and it's actions". It is somewhat like "the operating system" of the organization. "It guides how employees think, act and feel."

Organization culture has been defined, by scholars in varied ways and numerous definition of culture have been proposed. A few of these insights are:

Porter, Lawler & Hackman (1975) identify organization culture as:

"A set of customs and typical patterns of ways of doing things. The force, pervasiveness and nature of such model, beliefs and values vary considerably from organization to organization. Yet it is assumed that an organization that has any history at all has developed some sort of culture and that this will have a vital impact on the degree of success of any effort to improve or alter the organization."

Edgar H. Schein (1984) defines organization culture as:

"A set of basic assumptions that a given group has invented, discovered or developed in learning to cope with its problems of external adaptations and internal integration that have worked well enough to be considered valid, and therefore, to be taught to new members as a

correct way to percieve, think and feel in relation to these problems."

According to Daniel R. Denison (1990):

"Organization culture refers to the underlying values, beliefs and principles that serve as a foundation for organization's management systems, as well as the set of management practices and behaviors that both exemplify and reinforce those basic principles."

Thus, though organization culture is defined by different people in different ways, most of the definitions stress on the importance of shared norms and values in the study of culture. The core of the culture is formed by values which are not visible but shared by people even when membership in the group changes. Organization culture has many characteristics. Based on the varied definitions of culture, Amarchand (1992) identified the following seven distinct characteristics of organization culture. Culture is -

- Learned
- Rooted in the traditions of the organization
- Shared by the people of the organization
- Transgenerational
- Cumulative
- Symbolic in nature
- Multifaceted (i.e. it is composed of several elements put together).

A critical examination of the deliberations presented above seems to suggest that culture determines the important issues within the organization. It identifies the principal goals, work methods and behaviours, work rules, individual interaction patters in which they address each other and the ways in which personal relationships are conducted. Sinha (1980) identified that in complex organizations there may be subcultures, which may be different from each other. Different units of a corporate body may develop different cultures. In the same organization, finance, production, marketing, personnel and maintenance groups may hold different values and world-views and hence, while sharing parts of the organization culture, these may have different specific patterns.

3.3.2 Organizational Culture and Leadership/ E-Leadership

One way of uncovering the relationship between culture and leadership is to examine how culture has been conceptualized in organizational theory. Smircich (1983) identifies two approaches to the study of the cultural phenomenon in organizations: culture as an organizational variable and culture seen as something that can be manipulated. Thus the nature, direction, and impact of such manipulation are dependent on the skills and abilities of the leader. The majority of the literature which extols the virtues of transformational leadership demonstrates widespread support for this view (for example, Nicholls, 1988; Quick, 1992; Simms, 1997).

In contrast, if culture is seen as an integral part of the organization, then the thinking, feeling, and responses of leaders are moulded by the culture (Bass and Avolio, 1993; Schein, 1992).

Schein (1992) observes that organizational culture and leadership are intertwined. He illustrates this inter-connection by looking at the relationship between leadership and culture in the context of the organizational life cycle. Thus, during the process of organizational formation, the founder of a company creates an organization which reflects their values and beliefs. In this sense, the founder creates and shapes the cultural traits of their organization. However, as the organization develops and time passes, the created culture of the organization exerts an influence on the leader and shapes the actions and style of the leader. Through this dynamic ongoing process, the leader creates and is in turn shaped by the organizational culture. In summarizing the consensus of opinion on the links between organizational culture and leadership, Bass and Avolio (1993) mirror the argument of Schein (1992) by suggesting that the relationship between the two concepts represents an ongoing interplay in which the leader shapes the culture and is in turn shaped by the resulting culture.

Bass (1985) demonstrates the relationship between leadership and culture by examining the impact of different styles of leadership on culture. He argues that transactional leaders tend to operate within the confines and limits of the existing culture, while transformational leaders frequently work towards changing the organizational culture in line with their vision. Similarly, some of the studies have observed that good leaders need to develop the skills that enable them to alter aspects of their culture in order to improve their organizational performance.

While there is no shortage of claims that leadership and culture are linked in the literature (Bass and Avolio, 1993; Nicholls, 1988; Quick, 1992; Schein, 1992; Simms, 1997), there have been very few empirical examinations of the nature and performance implications of this link. One exception is a recent study of organizational change in the United States federal civil service. Hennessey concludes that leadership played a major role in nurturing the appropriate organizational culture which helped to improve the implementation of specific government reforms. Hennessey (1998) further argues that 'the most effective leaders foster, support, and sustain organizational cultures that facilitate the type of management reform envisioned by "reinventing government" and the attendant increases in effectiveness and efficiency'.

3.4 Commitment

3.4.1 Commitment as a Concept

Among various forms of attitudes, commitment has gained substantial interest among organizational behavior researchers. Its significance stems from the belief that committed employees will demonstrate differential degree of organizational outcomes such as employee turnover, employee performance, and their intention to stay or leave an organization (Meyer and Allen 1997).

In the study of organizational behavior, organizational commitment is the extent of an individual's commitment to an organization. There are three major types of organizational commitment. According to Meyer and Allen (1997), the three-component model of commitment which has been well researched and is widely accepted by the academic community include-

- **Affective Commitment:** Affective commitment refers to employees' emotional attachment to identification with, and involvement in the organization. Employees with a strong degree of affective commitment continue employment with the organization because they want to do so. In this case, an individual strongly identifies with the goals of the organization and desires to remain a part of the organization. This is the ideal 'happy' state for an individual.
- **Continuance Commitment:** The individual remains with an organization because of a perceived loss of sunk costs. The individual believes that he has invested a great deal of effort/time and has to remain in the organization. Continuance commitment refers to an awareness of the costs associated with leaving the organization. Employees whose primary link to the organization is based on continuance commitment remain because they need to do so.

- **Normative Commitment:** The individual remains with an organization because of feelings of obligation. For instance, the organization may have invested resources in training an employee who then feels obliged to stay with the organization to 'repay the debt.' Employees with a high degree or level of normative commitment feel that they ought to remain with the organization.

Conceptually, organizational commitment has been defined in various ways. A plethora of definitions found in commitment literature is shown below:

According to Kanter (1968) Commitment is:

"The attachment of an individual's fund of affectivity and emotion to the group."

Hall, Schneider and Nygren (1970) described Commitment as:

"The process by which the goals of the organization and those of the individual become increasingly integrated or congruent."

Hrebiniak and Alutto (1972) stated that Commitment is:

"A structural phenomenon which occurs as a result of individual-organizational transactions and alterations in side-bets or investments over time."

Buchanan (1974) concludes Commitment as:

"A partisan, affective attachment to the goals and values of the organization to one's role in relation to goals and values, and to the organization for its own sake, apart from its purely instrumental worth."

According to Mowday, Porter and Steers (1982) Commitment is:

"The relative strength of an individual's identification with and involvement in a particular organization."

Steers (1997) concedes that:

"Organizational Commitment can be defined as the relative strength of an individual's identification with and involvement in a particular organization."

A scrutiny of these definitions reveals the inconsistency underlying the understanding and perception. of the concept of commitment among researchers. In their review of the conceptualization of commitment, Mathieu and Zajac (1990) suggested that these definitions signify a unidimensional nature of the concept.

Allen and Meyer (1991) went further to propose that commitment, instead, should be conceived as multidimensional in nature.

Pfeffer (1998) and Wood and Albanese (1995) argue that commitment is a core variable. Commitment has been described as:

- **Attitudinal Commitment:** that is loyalty and support for the organization, strength of identification with the organization (Porter 1985), a belief in its values and goals and a readiness to put in effort for the organization.
- **Behavioural Commitment:** actually remaining with the company and continuing to pursue its objectives.

Porter, Steers Mowday and Boulian (1974) suggested that it has three primary components:

- A strong belief in and acceptance of the organization's goals and values.
- A willingness to exert considerable effort on behalf of the organization.
- A strong desire to remain with the organization.

A critical examination of the thoughts presented above seems to suggest that organizational commitment is one of those concepts that are used in a number of different ways. In most cases we use the term to refer to a type of employee, that is, an employee with high organizational commitment. We generally refer to three observable patterns of behavior. When we see an employee exhibiting these patterns of behavior, we attribute these patterns to something we call commitment and we say that individual is committed. More recently, these behaviors have been termed organizational citizenship behaviors. The three components of commitment are:

- Identification with the organization's goals and/or mission manifested in pride in and defense of the organization
- Long-term membership in the organization and intention to remain with the organization, often termed loyalty
- High levels of extra role behavior, that is, behaviour beyond required performance

3.4.2 Commitment and Leadership/ E-Leadership

A review of organizational commitment literature shows that two classes of variables, individual and organizational, have been used as antecedents of organizational commitment. The individual and demographic variables commonly comprise of age, sex, tenure, income, marital status and education. These demographic variables are presumed to cause commitment because through employee's actions, they make some reward-producing arrangements, the result of which leaves them committed to the organizations (Becker, 1960). The organizational variables comprise of task characteristics, pay, supervision, opportunities for advancement, etc. In this view, organizational commitment is the result of what happens to employees in organizations. It is a form of psychological contract employees make in response to the benefits provided by the organizations (Angle and Perry, 1983).

In has been also found that the commitment factor was related to performance and included items that asked subjects about how enthusiastic they were about trying for their goal. This emotion-focused factor not only was a more valid predictor of performance but showed higher variance than the more cognitively focused factors containing items which simply asked subjects whether they were committed to their organization or not.

Meta-analytic review for organizational commitment reports 124 published studies (Mathieu and Zajac, 1990) covering 48 different variables as antecedents, correlates and consequences. Broad groupings include personal variables, role stress, job characteristic, group relations and organizational variables as antecedents, motivation and job-satisfaction as correlates and job performance and turnover as consequences. Of the personal variables only age, perceived personal competence and protestant work ethics were positively and significantly correlated with organizational commitment. Among job characteristics, skill variety, challenge and job scope were positively related to organizational commitment. Many group and leader linked variables were found related like task interdependence, leader initiating structure, leader consideration, leader communication and participative leadership. Role-ambiguity, role conflict and role-overload were negatively related to organizational commitment.

Sass and Canary (1991) propose that organizational commitment and identification are two constructs that communication researches currently utilize to study the employee-based relationship. A review of the literature reveals that the terms 'commitment' and 'identification' have distinct meanings although they have developed as virtual synonyms. The review indicates that contemporary conceptualization and operationalisation of attitudinal commitment and identification as product refer to the same cluster of attitude. An empirical study with 122 employees (aged 22-66 years) found that commitment and identification correlated consistently and significantly with relevant attitudinal variables, tenure and demographic variables. For this reason communication scholars have been advised to refer to identification as a process and commitment as outcome of that process.

Aryee, Wyatt and Min (1991) worked on organizational professional conflict with 245 years old professional accountancy firm in Singapore. Questionnaire measured organizational commitment, professional commitment, skill utilization, realizations of professional expectations, job satisfaction and turnover intentions. Multiple regression analysis was performed for the entire sample and then for professional (i.e. accounting firms) and non-professional employment settings. In general, the findings provided support for the congruity thesis. Job satisfaction, realization of professional expectations and professional-commitment contributed to professional organizational commitment. Skill utilization emerged as a significant predictor variable in non-professional setting. Organizational commitment and job satisfaction are the main predictors of human intentions.

Wallace (1993) assessed the nature of relations between professional commitment and organizational commitment by using meta-analysis to integrate findings of correlational data from 15 published studies. Results indicated a moderately strong, positive association between professional and organizational commitment. Investigation of four potential moderators revealed that the degree of occupational professionalism, the individual's position in the organization and the form of professional commitment had moderating effects on the true correlation between professional and organizational commitment.

Cantor and Mischel (1979) found commitment to be an attribute on which individuals evaluate others and that commitment was distinct from other personal characteristics such as extraversion.

Much research literature focuses on ways of developing and enhancing commitment among employees (Mowday, Porter, and Steers, 1982) suggesting that organizations view commitment as a desirable attribute. Support for this perspective is shown by studies linking commitment with a variety of work behaviors, including voluntary turnover (Mowday et al., 1982), employee performance (Meyer, Paunonen, Gellatly, Goffin, and Jackson, 1989), organizational citizenship (O'Reilly and Chatman, 1986; Shore & Wayne, 1993), and absenteeism (Mowday et al., 1982). Despite extensive research on commitment, managerial perceptions of employee commitment have not yet been examined. Rather, all prior studies have been based on employee self-reports of commitment. However, as organizational representatives, managers in all likelihood make attributions about the commitment of their employees. These attributions may well affect the managers' allocation of rewards.

Feldman's (1981, 1986) work on cognitive processes provides a framework for understanding the development of managerial assessments of employee commitment. According to Feldman, person categorization occurs very early in the relationship between an employee and a supervisor and is essential to perception, information storage, and organization.

The 2005 What's Working survey, conducted by Mercer Human Resource Consulting LLC in the first quarter of this year, found that two of every three workers say they feel a strong sense of commitment to their organizations. But there was much in the survey's findings to suggest that companies' leaders are not winning the confidence of the troops.

Darling and Box (1999) found that it was through effective leadership strategies for customer care, product and process innovation, and committed people, that each of the top leaders had achieved successful business results.

A recent development in the leadership area has been the interest in transformational and charismatic leadership (Conger and Kanungo, 1987, 1988; Kuhnert and Lewis, 1987). House (1977) proposed a theory of charismatic leadership that focused on how a leader can create an impression among subordinates that the leader has the competence and vision to achieve success. The result is an enthusiasm and commitment by subordinates to the group objectives.

According to Bass, 1985; Yukl, 1989 the transformational leader gains a greater commitment from subordinates and induces them to transcend personal self-interest for the betterment of the group or organization not only with charisma but also by serving as a coach, teacher, or mentor.

There is evidence transformational leaders enhance follower effort, satisfaction, commitment, and performance (Lowe, Kroeck, and Sivasubramaniam, 1996; Podsakoff, MacKenzie, Moorman, and Fetter, 1990; Yammarino, Spangler, and Bass, 1993).

Research of charismatic leadership has consistently found significant relationships with follower trust, effort, and commitment (Howell and Frost, 1989; Lowe et al., 1996).

3.5 Performance

3.5.1 Performance as a Concept

Performance can simply be defined as "focused behavior" or "purposeful work" (Rudman, 1998). That is, jobs exist to achieve specific and defined results (outputs) and people are employed so that organizations can achieve those results. Thus, performance is what organizations need from employees to achieve their goals. Performance should not be confused with activity. For example, meetings, operating machines, etc. are work activities. These activities must be put into context with what the organization wants employees to do, and how well. Thus, focused behavior that achieves purposeful results is considered "optimal" performance.

When the "actual" performance does not meet the "optimal" performance, then a "performance gap" occurs (optimal - actual = gap). If this gap between actual performance and optimal performance starts to have an adverse impact, then it may be thought of as "poor" performance: specific, agreed-upon deviations from expected behavior (Mitchell and O'Reilly, 1983). Note that deviations must be defined and agreed upon by both the evaluator and the performer.

An output occurs in every organization system and the processes within it. Outputs are built by people, technology, materials, information, and time. Performance can cause two types of impact (or result) upon the output:

- **Positive Impact:** The performance, combined with time, material, information, and technology cause a "desired impact" upon the output. In turn, the output cues the performer to the adjustments that must be made, which further provides a positive impact upon the outcome. Hence, performance not only affects the output, the output also affects the performance.
- **Negative Impact:** Any gap in the optimal performance cause an "unwanted impact" upon the output. The gap may be caused by the lack of training, environmental factors, motivators, etc. In turn, this performance gap has a negative impact (inverse relationship) upon the output that miscues the performer, which in turn, further compounds the problem.

Gilbert (1998) said that performance has two aspects -- behavior being the means and its consequence being the end.

Managing performance has the dual purpose of 1) arranging situations (environment) so that employees can do their best and 2) growing the employees by educating, enlightening, and appreciating them. Its purpose is to achieve specific and defined results from people so that the organization can achieve its goals and objectives.

It is much easier to fix situations by making structural changes to the organization, rather than trying to fix or change people. These include such means as changing reporting relationships, enlarging the job, improving a process, or opening lines of communication.

Once performance barriers have been removed, employees can be educated, enlightened, and appreciated. This assumption is based on the premise that most employees try to do their best. They prefer harmony over conflict, action over inaction, and productivity over delays (Farson, 1996). We often refuse to believe this as most studies on human behavior are performed on people when they are not at their best, such as in school, clinics, or prison. Thus, most studies on human behavior are performed in the process of trying to "reform" people.

3.5.2 Performance and Leadership/ E-Leadership

Conventional views of organizational leadership have generally assumed that leaders have a significant and possibly crucial impact on the performance of the organizations they head, but this 'individualist' view has been increasingly questioned by "contextualists," who emphasize the constraints that are placed on leaders by situational factors (Hall, 1977; Pfeffer and Salancik, 1978). Although there have been few studies that have a direct bearing on this important issue, research on sports organizations (Grusky, 1963; Gamson and Scotch, 1964; Eitzen and Yetman, 1972; Allen, Panian, and Lotz, 1979), governmental institutions (Salancik and Pfeffer, 1977), and industrial organizations (Lieberson and O'Connor, 1972; Samuelson, Gaibraith, and McGuire, 1985) has tended to support the contextualist position. In practice, however, the contextualist argument has rested heavily on the findings of just one major study, that of Lieberson and O'Connor (1972), which has become the most commonly, cited evidence of the "inertial" organization (Hambrick and Mason, 1984) and which is widely regarded as the major counterpoint to the proposition that leadership makes a difference.

Pearce, Stevenson, and Perry (1985) noted that "the appointment of new corporation presidents can make headlines in the business sections of the newspapers, but Lieberson and O'Connor (1972) found leadership change to have no effect on organizational indicators such as profits. Similarly, Hambrick and Mason (1984) stated that in comparison with the effects of other independent variables, the apparent added effect of leadership was nil.

Pfeffer and Salancik (1978) commented that studies estimating the effect of administrators have found them to account for about 10 percent of the variance in organizational performance which is a striking contrast to the 90 percent of intellectual effort that has been devoted to developing theories of individual action. Leadership, it seems, doesn't make a difference.

Weiner's (1978) replication study showed that the percentages of performance variance accounted for by the independent variables are highly sensitive to the order in which they are treated. The impact of leadership appears either to be substantial or negligible purely as a consequence of its being assessed first or last.

Leaders high in transformational behaviors achieve maximum performance from followers because they are able to inspire followers to raise their criteria for success and develop innovative problem solving skills (Bass, 1985; Yammarino and Bass, 1990).

Fiedler (1996), one of the most respected researchers on leadership, has provided a recent treatise on the importance of leadership by arguing that the effectiveness of a leader is a major determinant of the success or failure of a group, organization, or even an entire country. Indeed, it has been argued that one way in which organizations have sought to cope with the increasing volatility and turbulence of the external environment is by training and developing leaders and equipping them with the skills to cope (Darcy and Kleiner, 1991; Hennessey, 1998; Saari et al., 1988). These claims are based on the assumption of a direct link between leadership and organizational performance.

Widely celebrated cases of a direct leadership–performance link may be found in numerous anecdotal accounts of improvements of company performance attributed to changes in leadership (see, for example, Nicholls, 1988; Quick, 1992; Simms, 1997). However, empirical studies into the links between leadership and performance have been lacking. One notable exception is the detailed study of the impact of leadership on performance in the somewhat surprising context of Icelandic fishing ships. Thorlindsson (1987) suggests that variations in the performance of different fishing ships, under identical conditions can be accounted for by the leadership skills of captains. Over a three-year period, Thorlindsson (1987) revealed that the leadership qualities of the ship captains accounted for 35 to 49 per cent of variation in the catch of different crews.

Other studies which examine the links between leadership and performance coincide with the re-emergence of the 'one best way to lead' debate. Of particular relevance is the resurgence of interest into charismatic leadership, which is frequently referred to as transformational leadership (Bass and Avolio, 1993). A number of researchers theorize that transformational leadership is linked to organizational performance (for example, Bycio et al., 1995; Howell and Avolio, 1993). Conceptually, it is argued that the visionary and inspirational skills of transformational leaders motivate followers to deliver superior performance (Nicholls, 1988; Quick, 1992).

In summary, much of the above evidence presented as supporting the claim of a leadership–performance link is anecdotal and frequently over-concentrates on the 'transformational' role of leaders in corporate successes (for example, Quick, 1992; Simms, 1997; Taffinder, 1995). It would appear that few studies have responded to the observation of Porter and Mckibbin (1988) that much of the research reported as supporting this claim is either inconclusive or empirically suspect.

According to Collins and Porras (1994), factors associated with performance are organizing arrangements; social factors; physical setting; technology; leadership; products and services; vision; financial analysis; markets and environment.

Tvorik and McGivern (1997) showed that areas that contribute to performance are organizational alignment and culture; organizational resources; organizational capabilities and learning; industry structure and strategic groups; leadership and vision.

Bass (1985) extended charismatic leadership to the theory of transformational leadership where the leader is able to inspire and activate subordinates to perform beyond expectations and to achieve goals beyond those normally set. The theory posits that the transformational leader achieves greater than expected performance through any one of three interrelated ways: (a) an increased level of awareness by subordinates about the importance of designated outcomes, (b) by getting individuals to transcend their own self-interest for the sake of the team, and (c) by altering the subordinates' need levels on Maslow's hierarchy or expanding the set of needs.

A laboratory study by Howell and Frost (1989) also found participants who worked under a charismatic leader to have high task performance.

Studies have found high levels of peak performance under transformational leadership (Stoner-Zemel, 1988) and high correlation between charismatic leadership and effectiveness (Seltzer and Bass, 1987).

Howell (1986) also found increased productivity of a charismatic leader's group and improvement in individual performance for subordinates of transformational leaders.

There is evidence that transformational leaders enhance follower effort, satisfaction, commitment, and performance (Lowe, Kroeck, and Sivasubramaniam, 1996; Podsakoff, MacKenzie, Moorman, and Fetter, 1990; Yammarino, Spangler, and Bass, 1993).

Leaders high in transformational behaviors achieve maximum performance from followers because they are able to inspire followers to raise their criteria for success and develop innovative problem solving skills (Bass, 1985; Yammarino and Bass, 1990).

4 RESEARCH METHODOLOGY

An attempt has been made to identify the impact of Information Technology on leadership. A comparison of business organizations with traditional leadership vis-à-vis e-leadership was undertaken so as to analyze the difference between the two. For this purpose five different organizations in BPO sector and three organizations in IT sector were chosen. This chapter discusses the research methodology that has been adopted for the study. The ensuing sections discuss the study's research design, questionnaire development, measures undertaken and statistical techniques used for data analysis.

4.1 Data Set

(A) Data Sources

The present research work is an empirical one based on both primary and secondary data. The theory is basically developed from secondary sources of information and a thorough study of various academic works in the field has been attempted. Various sources used in this connection are: books, doctoral theses and M.Phil dissertations, study reports and articles that appeared in journals and newspapers. Some of the journals read for this purpose include: Journal of Applied Psychology, Journal of Public administration Research and Theory, Organizational Dynamics, Academy of Management Review, Academy of management Journal, Organization Science etc. Primary data were collected with the help of a self administered questionnaire.

(B) Pilot Survey

The main objective of the study was to capture the impact of Information Technology on leadership. Therefore, the qualitative stage preceded the survey to identify the dimensions to be included in the questionnaire. The present study makes an attempt to customize the measurement instruments in relation to the study undertaken.

A pilot survey of 20 respondents was conducted in the initial phase. The sample was chosen on the basis of convenience sampling. The respondents were approached through e-mail and were simply asked to fill the questionnaire according to the instructions mentioned. The responses were carefully reviewed and after applying some statistical tools like average and correlation, subsequent changes were made in the questionnaire.

(C) Quantitative Phase: Questionnaire Development

Data collection was done through self-administered questionnaire, semi-structured interviews and availability of organizational records. The questionnaire consisted of 114 items, which were spread over personal profile of the respondents and other 5 sections (106 statements). Eight questions in the questionnaire related to personal profile of the respondents. Rest of the questionnaire was divided into five main sections.

As discussed above, items to be included in the final questionnaire were identified on the basis of the pilot survey.

The questionnaire comprised of six sections. To begin with, the respondents were asked to provide information relating to their background and personal aspects. Section A of the questionnaire pertained to items relating to trust level among the team members. Organizational Commitment related statements were incorporated in Section B. In Section C and D, Organizational Culture and Performance were studied respectively. Section E dealt with items measuring motivational level of the team members.

In addition, few open-ended questions relating to the subject of the study were included so as to gain a deeper insight.

(D) The Sample

For the present study, questionnaires were distributed to around 350 respondents, from whom 300 correctly completed questionnaires have been obtained, yielding a response rate of 85%. The high response rate is due to the use of 'personal-contact' approach followed by periodic follow-ups. Questionnaires were distributed to the team members personally and they were asked to contact the researcher whenever they encountered any difficulty in responding to the questionnaire. The respondents were asked to fill up the set of questions as per the instructions mentioned on it. They were specifically requested not to read all the items at once but to go through each individual statement and answer it and only then move on the next. All respondents were assured of the confidentiality of their responses and were encouraged to express their opinions freely and fairly. Wherever required, the questionnaire was explained by the researcher personally in a vernacular language and was filled personally.

The sample of 300 respondents was considered of sufficient size to provide the needed reliability and validity to the research study. The research design incorporated non-probability sampling based on convenience. According to Churchill (1979), this type of sampling can be adopted when the emphasis is on exploratory research.

Sample consisted of 300 respondents working in five different BPO organizations and three IT companies. Distribution of sample is as shown in Table 4.1:

Table 4.1: Distribution of Sample

Sl. No.	*Sector*	*No. of Respondents*	
		Leadership	***E-leadership***
1	BPO	153	56
2	IT	51	40
	Total	204	96

The study was based on convenience sampling. The sample consisted of teams of executives drawn from the companies. Approximately 6-7 teams under leadership and 3-4 teams under e-leadership were studied in each BPO company. Similarly 4-5 teams under leadership and 3-4 teams under e-leadership were studied in each IT company.

4.2 Measures used in the Study

The present study employed the following measures:

4.2.1 Measure of Personal Information

The personal profile included questions regarding the respondent's personal background and his job including age, sex, salary, experience in the present organization, education, marital status and position in the organization. The questionnaire was further divided in five parts.

The sample profile is presented in Table 4.2. The table categorizes the sample on the basis of age, marital status, sex, monthly family income, occupation, and education.

Table 4.2: Sample Profile

Basic Classification	***No. of Respondents***	***%age***	***Valid %age***	***Cumulative %age***
BPO Organizations	209	69.7	69.7	69.7
IT Organizations	91	30.3	30.3	100.0
Age				
20 years and less	6	2.0	2.0	2.0
21-25 Years	218	72.7	72.7	74.7
26-30 years	66	22.0	22.0	96.7
31-35 years	10	3.3	3.3	100.0
Marital Status				
Married	250	83.3	86.8	86.8
Unmarried	38	12.7	13.2	100.0
Missing	12	4.0		
Monthly Income				
Less than 20,000	180	60.0	76.3	76.3
20,001—25,000	30	10.0	12.7	89.0
25,001—30,000	15	5.0	6.4	95.3
Above 30,000	11	3.7	4.7	100.0
Missing	64	21.3		
Education				
BE/B.Tech	63	21.0	21.2	21.2
M. Tech	3	1.0	1.0	22.2
MBA	24	8.0	8.1	30.3
MCA	31	10.3	10.4	40.7
Diploma/ Certificate	7	2.3	2.4	43.1
Post graduate	28	9.3	9.4	52.5
Graduate	133	44.3	44.8	97.3
12th Pass	8	2.7	2.7	100.0
Missing	3	1.0		

Work Experience				
Less than 2 years	103	34.3	34.6	34.6
2-5 years	161	53.7	54.0	88.6
5-10 years	34	11.3	11.4	100.0
Missing	2	.7		

(i) Sector

A total of 209 respondents were from the BPO sector and 91 were from IT sector.

(ii) Age

The sample profile shows that majority of the respondents are in the age group of 21-25 years (constituting 72.7% of the total sample) followed by respondents within the age bracket of 26-30 years (22%).

(iii) Marital Status

Of the total sample of 300 respondents, 83.3% were unmarried and 12.7% were married.

(iv) Monthly Income

The personal information provided by the respondents show that 60% of them belong to the income group of less than 20,000 Rupees per month. While 10% of the respondents earn with in a range of 20,001- 25,000 Rs. per month, only 26 respondents earn more than Rs. 25000/-. Out of the total respondents, 64 people did not mention about their monthly income.

(v) Education

Table 4.1 shows that 44.3% respondents are graduates and 21% are engineers. MBAs contributed to 8% of the total respondents.

(vi) Work Experience

As for as work experience of the sample, maximum number of respondents fall in the range of 2-5 years followed by 34.3% of respondents with a work experience of less than 2 years.

4.2.2 Operationalization of the Variables

Measures needed for the study were Trust, Commitment, Organizational culture, Performance and Motivation. The different scales used to measure the various variables were as following:

(A) Measure of Trust

A part of the Trust scale developed by Jack R. Gibb in 1972 was used for the purpose of identifying the Trust level among team members. A pilot study was conducted to test the scale. Finally the scale consisting of 12 items has been used in the study.

The 12 item scale contained six reversed score items. The items were scored on a five-point scale with the following label:

1. Strongly Disagree
2. Disagree
3. Undecided
4. Agree
5. Strongly Agree.

(B) Measure of Commitment

The scale used for the purpose of measuring the affective responses of the employees was the one developed by Buchanan in 1974.

Buchanan (1974) views commitment as a "partisan, affective attachment to the goals and values of an organization, to one's role in relation to goals and values, and to the organization for its own sake, apart from its purely instrumental worth". The concept is, therefore, measured through three components.

(a)Job Identification is viewed as adopting as one's own the goal and values of the organization. It is tapped through six items, which are drawn from Hall Schneider and Nygren (1970).

(b)Job Involvement is measured through five items from Lodahl and Kejner (1965). These are intended to measure psychological immersion or absorption in the activities of one's work role.

(c) Organizational Loyalty is a response that tries to tap the feelings of affection and attachment to the organization and is measured with the help of seven items.

The 18 item scale contained five reversed score items. Buchanan obtained responses from 279 managers from eight organizations and coefficient alphas of 0.86, 0.84, 0.92 and 0.94 were recorded for the three sub-scales and the total scale respectively. The sub-scales were found to be inter co-related. The correlation between Identification and Involvement was 0.65, between Identification and Loyalty was 0.74, and between Involvement and Loyalty was 0.58.

The scale had 18 items. The representation of different components according to the item number is given below. (R) following an item number depicts that the score needed to be reversed for that item.

Identification:	1, 2, 3, 4, 5, 6
Involvement:	7, 8, (R) 9, 10, 11(R)
Loyalty:	12 (R), 13, 14 (R), 15, 16 (R), 17, 18.

The items were scored on a five- point scale according to the following response categories:

1. Strongly Disagree
2. Disagree
3. Undecided
4. Agree
5. Strongly Agree.

(C) Measure of Organizational Culture

For the purpose of measuring the organizational culture, the Organizational Climate Questionnaire (OCQ) by Adrian Furnham and Leonard D. Goodstein, 1997 was used.

The scale had 55 items. The representation of different components according to item number is given below:

1. Role Clarity : 1 to 9
2. Communication : 10 to 21
3. Reward System : 22 to 31
4. Career Development : 32 to 41
5. Innovation : 42 to 46
6. Teamwork and Support : 47 to 55.

The items were scored on a five-point scale according to the following response categories:

1. Strongly Disagree
2. Disagree
3. Undecided
4. Agree
5. Strongly Agree.

(D) Measure of Performance

The scale developed by Pam Jones and Joy Palmer (1996) had 12 items. The representation of different components according to item number is given below:

1. Purpose : 1,2,3,4
2. Performance : 5,6,7,8
3. Learning : 9,10,11,12.

The items were scored on a five-point scale according to the following response categories:

1. Strongly Disagree
2. Disagree
3. Undecided

4. Agree
5. Strongly Agree.

(E) Measure of Motivation

The scale had 9 items as developed by M. S. Shookla (2004). The items were scored on a five-point scale according to the following response categories:

1. Strongly Disagree
2. Disagree
3. Undecided
4. Agree
5. Strongly Agree.

4.3 Method of Data Analysis

The data obtained from the survey were coded and fed into computer. This included processing, coding, tabulation and analysis of data. SPSS package was used for analysis. Statistical techniques like mean scores, standard deviation, t-test were used in the analysis. This is followed by the presentation and interpretation of the results along with their managerial implications and concluding notes.

For preparing data for computation, data definition file was prepared with variable numbers, column numbers, variable codes and labels. All the 106 items of this questionnaire were indexed into 16 variables for final analysis and these are referred to as given below in Table 4.3.

Table 4.3: Indexing of the Variables under Study for the Analysis

Variable No.	*Variable Label*	*Variables*
1.	TR	Trust
2	CM	Commitment
3.	ID	Identification
4.	IN	Involvement

5.	LO	Loyalty
6.	OC	Organizational Culture
7.	RC	Role Clarity
8.	CO	Communication
9.	RS	Reward System
10.	CD	Career Development
11.	INN	Innovation
12.	TAS	Teamwork and Support
13.	PU	Purpose
14.	PER	Performance
15.	LG	Learning
16.	MOT	Motivation

4.4 Statistical Treatment of the Data

After scoring the questionnaire, the raw data was tabulated for each variable being studied separately for each organization. The computation of the raw data was done in order to do the following statistical analysis:

1. Descriptive Analysis
2. Inferential Analysis
3. Correlational analysis
4. Multiple Regression Analysis.

4.4.1 Descriptive Analysis

It was basically done with an objective of analyzing the mean scores and the standard deviation scores of the BPO companies, IT companies and the overall sample as well.

4.4.2 Inferential Analysis

The inferential statistics which included the 't-test', was computed to determine whether significant differences existed between the leadership and e-leadership on various dimensions viz. Trust, Commitment, Organizational Culture, Motivation and Performance.

4.4.3 Correlational Analysis

In order to understand the relationship among various variables taken for leadership and e-leadership under the study, the Pearson's product moment correlation was computed.

4.4.4 Multiple Regression Analysis

Regression is the determination of statistical relationship between two or more variables. Organizational Culture (one of the dimension of leadership/ e-leadership) was taken as dependent or criterion variable and remaining variables were taken as independent or predictor variables. The stepwise Multiple Regression was used (Bock, 1975).

5 RESULTS AND ANALYSIS

After scoring the questionnaire, the raw data were analyzed in different stages in order to study the formulated objectives as mentioned in the earlier chapters. The findings of the study are based on qualitative and quantitative analysis of the data relating to the selected variables of the study. The quantitative and qualitative results of the findings of different statistical techniques, used according to the objectives of the study, are depicted in the present chapter along with the discussions on findings.

Statistical Tools Used

Different statistical tools and techniques used for the study are:

1. Means
2. Standard Deviation
3. t-Test
4. Correlational Analysis
5. Multiple Regression Analysis

5.1 Descriptive Statistics

Descriptive statistics are used to describe the basic features of the data in a study. They provide simple summaries about the sample and the measures. Together with simple graphic analysis, they form the basis of virtually every quantitative analysis of data. With descriptive statistics we simply describe what is or what the data shows.

5.1.1 BPO Sector

The summary of the means and standard deviation of dimensions under leadership and e-leadership in BPO Sector (comprising of five companies) is presented in Table 5.1.1a and 5.1.1b respectively. The comparison of mean scores and standard deviation of dimensions under leadership and e-leadership in BPO sector i.e., Trust, Commitment, Organizational Culture, Performance and Motivation have also been plotted and presented in Charts 5.1, 5.2, 5.3, 5.4 and 5.5 respectively.

The results show that Trust in leadership in BPO Sector has a mean score of 3.06 with a standard deviation of 0.24. Commitment shows a mean score of 3.61 and standard deviation of 0.32. In case of other dimensions i.e., Organizational Culture, Performance and Motivation a little high mean score is seen as compared to Trust and Commitment. i.e., a value of 4.06, 4.11 and 4.07 respectively. Likewise, standard deviation of 0.45, 0.45, and 0.49 is seen for Organizational Culture, Performance and Motivation respectively.

As per Table 5.1.1a Performance under traditional leadership in BPO sector has the highest mean score while Trust has least mean score with least standard deviation.

Table 5.1.1b shows the mean scores and standard deviation of dimensions under e-leadership in BPO sector.

The table shows that mean score of Trust in e-leadership in BPO sector is 3.02 with a standard deviation of 0.35. Mean score for Commitment is 3.46 and standard deviation of 0.38. In case of Organizational Culture, the standard deviation is 0.52 with a mean score of 3.99. Performance and Motivation shows a mean score of 4.05 and 4.06 respectively. Standard deviation is 0.56 and 0.58 for Performance and Motivation respectively.

As per Table 5.1b Motivation under e-leadership in BPO sector has the highest mean score with highest standard deviation while Trust has least mean score with least standard deviation.

Table 5.1.1a: Mean Scores and Standard Deviation of Dimensions under Leadership in BPO Sector

Sl. No.	*Dimension*	*Mean*	*Standard Deviation*
1	Trust	3.06	0.24
2	Commitment	3.61	0.32
3	Organization Culture	4.06	0.45
4	Performance	4.11	0.45
5	Motivation	4.07	0.49

Table 5.1.1b: Mean Scores and Standard Deviation of Dimensions under E-Leadership in BPO Sector

Sl. No.	*Dimension*	*Mean*	*Standard Deviation*
1	Trust	3.02	0.35
2	Commitment	3.46	0.38
3	Organization Culture	3.99	0.52
4	Performance	4.05	0.56
5	Motivation	4.06	0.58

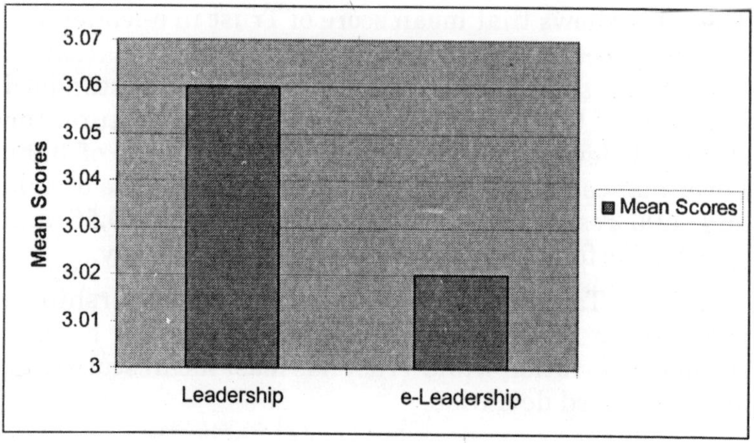

Chart 5.1: Comparison of Mean Scores for Trust under Leadership and E-Leadership in BPO Sector

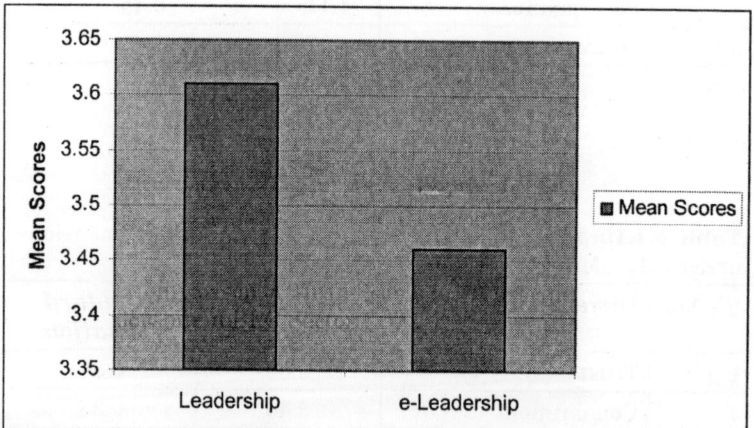

Chart 5.2: Comparison of Mean Scores for Commitment under Leadership and E-Leadership in BPO Sector

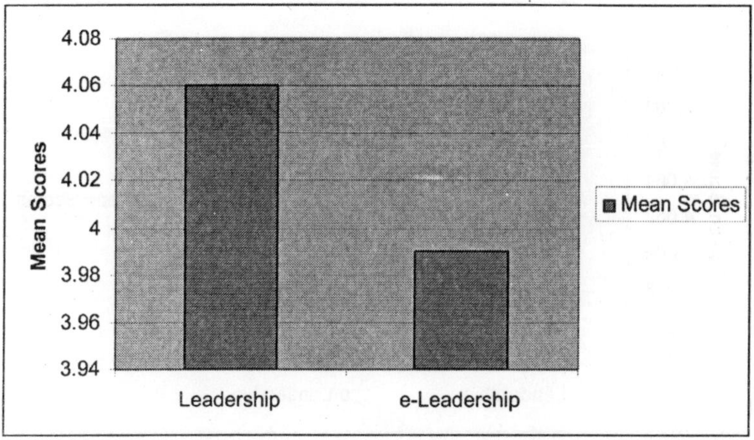

Chart 5.3: Comparison of Mean Scores for Organizational Culture under Leadership and E-Leadership in BPO Sector

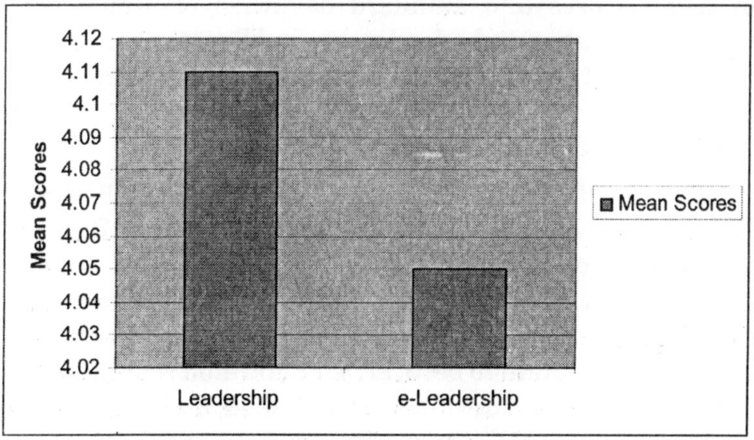

Chart 5.4: Comparison of Mean Scores for Performance under Leadership and E-Leadership in BPO Sector

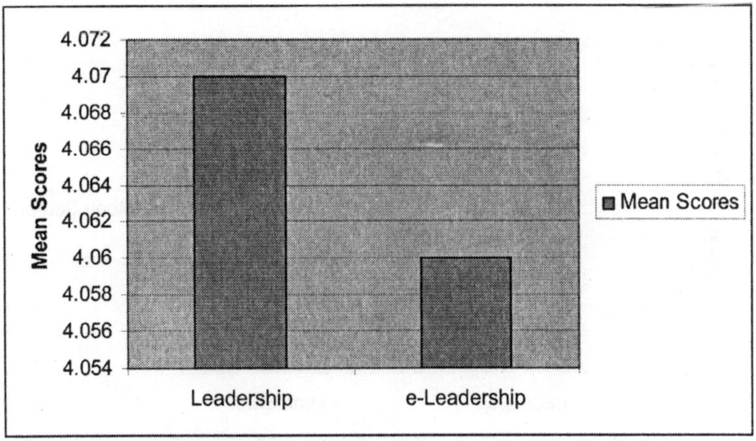

Chart 5.5: Comparison of Mean Scores for Motivation under Leadership and E-Leadership in BPO Sector

5.1.2 IT Sector

The summary of the means and standard deviation of dimensions under leadership and e-leadership in IT sector (comprising of three companies) is presented in Table 5.1.2a and 5.1.2b respectively. The comparison of mean scores and standard deviation of dimensions under leadership and e-leadership in IT sector i.e., Trust, Commitment, Organizational Culture, Performance and Motivation have also been plotted and presented in Chart 5.6, 5.7, 5.8, 5.9 and 5.10 respectively.

The results show that Trust in leadership in IT Sector has a mean score of 3.19 with a standard deviation of 0.38 while Commitment shows a mean score of 3.36 and standard deviation of 0.53. In case of other dimensions i.e., Organizational Culture, Performance and Motivation mean score is found to be. 3.77, 4.12 and 4.03 respectively. Likewise, standard deviation of 0.37, 0.49, and 0.52 is seen for Organizational Culture, Performance and Motivation respectively.

As per Table 5.1.2a Performance under traditional leadership in IT sector has the highest mean score while

Trust has least mean score. Commitment shows the highest standard deviation and Organizational Culture shows lowest standard deviation.

Table 5.1.2b shows the mean scores and standard deviation of dimensions under e-leadership in IT sector. The table shows that mean score of Trust under e-leadership in IT Sector is 3.12 with a standard deviation of 0.42. Mean score for Commitment is 3.27 with standard deviation of 0.61. In case of Organizational Culture the standard deviation is 0.65 with a mean score of 3.53. Performance and Motivation shows a mean score of 3.77 and 3.72 respectively. Standard deviation is 0.74 and 0.83 for Performance and Motivation respectively.

As per Table 5.1.2b, Performance under e-leadership in IT sector has the highest mean score while Trust has lowest mean value. The highest and lowest standard deviation is shown by Motivation and Trust respectively.

Table 5.1.2a: Mean Scores and Standard Deviation of Dimensions of Leadership under IT Sector

Sl. No.	*Dimension*	*Mean*	*Standard Deviation*
1	Trust	3.19	0.38
2	Commitment	3.36	0.53
3	Organization Culture	3.77	0.37
4	Performance	4.12	0.49
5	Motivation	4.03	0.52

Table 5.1.2b: Mean Scores and Standard Deviation of Dimensions under E-Leadership in IT Sector

Sl. No.	*Dimension*	*Mean*	*Standard Deviation*
1	Trust	3.12	0.42
2	Commitment	3.27	0.61
3	Organization Culture	3.53	0.65
4	Performance	3.77	0.74
5	Motivation	3.72	0.83

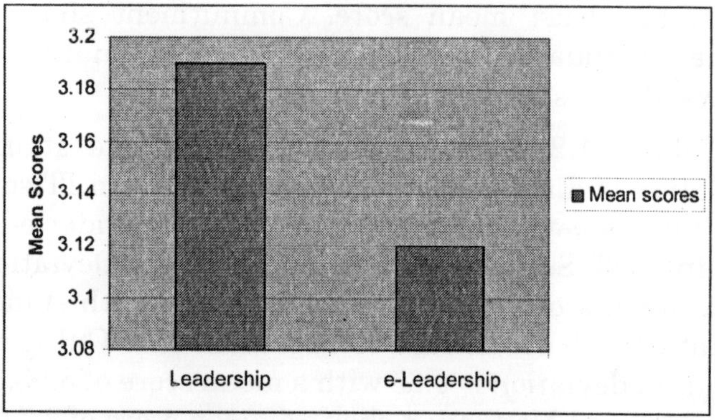

Chart 5.6: Comparison of Mean Scores for Trust under Leadership and E-Leadership in IT Sector

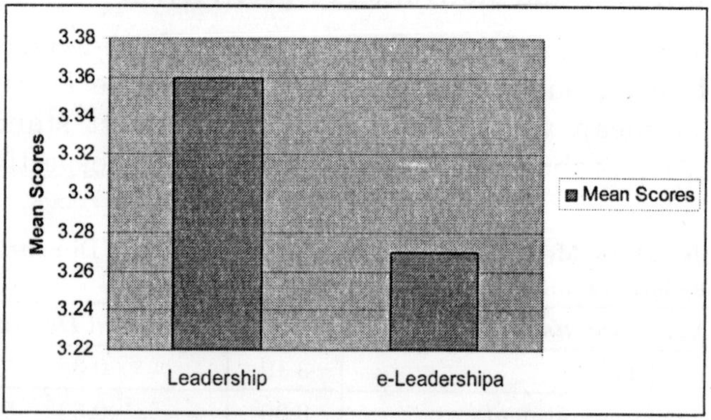

Chart 5.7: Comparison of Mean Scores for Commitment under Leadership and E-Leadership in IT Sector

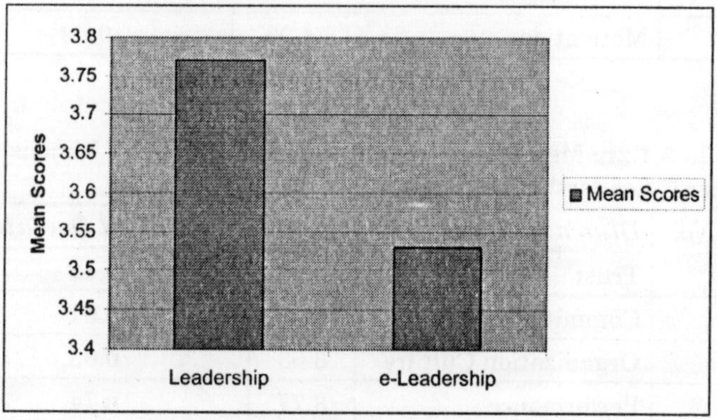

Chart 5.8: Comparison of Mean Scores for Organizational Culture under Leadership and E-Leadership in IT Sector

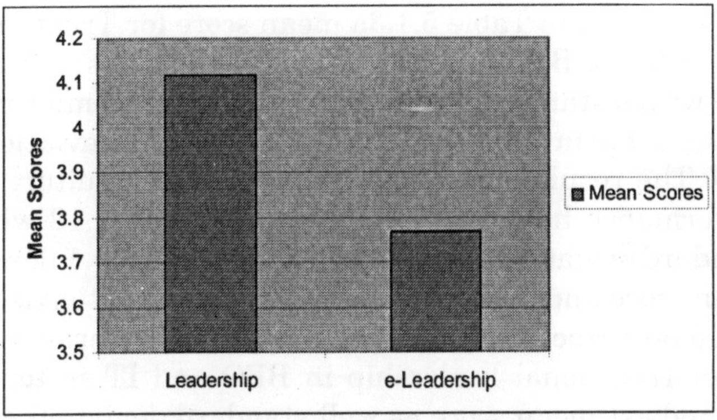

Chart 5.9: Comparison of Mean Scores for Performance under Leadership and E-Leadership in IT Sector

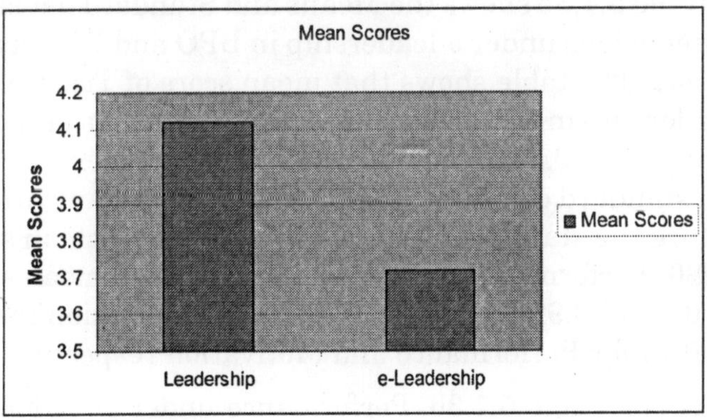

Chart 5.10: Comparison of Mean Scores for Performance under Leadership and E-Leadership in IT Sector

5.1.3 BPO + IT Sector

The summary of the means and standard deviation of dimensions under leadership and e-leadership in BPO and IT sector as a whole (comprising of eight companies) is presented in Table 5.3a and 5.3b respectively. The comparison of mean scores and standard deviation of dimensions under leadership and e-leadership in BPO and IT sector i.e., Trust, Commitment, Organizational Culture, Performance and Motivation has also been plotted and presented in Charts 5.11, 5.12, 5.13, 5.14 and 5.15 respectively.

According to Table 5.1.3a mean score for Trust under leadership in BPO and IT sector as a whole has a value of 3.10 with a standard deviation of 0.29 while Commitment shows a mean score of 3.55 and standard deviation of 0.40. The results show that Organizational Culture and Performance has a mean score of 3.99 and 4.12 with a standard deviation of 0.45 and 0.46 respectively. Likewise, mean score and standard deviation for Motivation is 4.06 and 0.50 respectively. As per table 5.1.3a, Performance under traditional leadership in BPO and IT sector has the highest mean score as well standard deviation while trust has least mean score as well standard deviation.

Table 5.1.3b shows the Means and Standard deviation of dimensions under e-leadership in BPO and IT sector as a whole. The table shows that mean score of Trust under e-leadership in BPO and IT sector is 3.06 with a standard deviation of 0.38. Mean score for Commitment is 3.38 with standard deviation of 0.50. In case of Organizational Culture the standard deviation is 0.71 with a mean score of 3.80. Performance and Motivation shows a mean score of 4.00 and 3.92 respectively. Standard deviation is 0.67 and 0.71 for Performance and Motivation respectively.

As per Table 5.1.3b, Performance under e-leadership in BPO and IT sector has the highest mean score while Trust has lowest mean value. The highest and lowest standard deviation is shown by Motivation and Trust respectively.

Table 5.1.3a: Mean Scores and Standard Deviation of Dimensions under Leadership in BPO and IT Sector as a Whole

Sl. No.	*Dimension*	*Mean*	*Standard Deviation*
1	Trust	3.10	0.29
2	Commitment	3.55	0.40
3	Organization Culture	3.99	0.45
4	Performance	4.12	0.46
5	Motivation	4.06	0.50

Table 5.1.3b: Mean Scores and Standard Deviation of Dimensions under E-Leadership in BPO and IT Sector as a Whole

Sl. No.	*Dimension*	*Mean*	*Standard Deviation*
1	Trust	3.06	0.38
2	Commitment	3.38	0.50
3	Organization Culture	3.80	0.71
4	Performance	4.00	0.67
5	Motivation	3.92	0.72

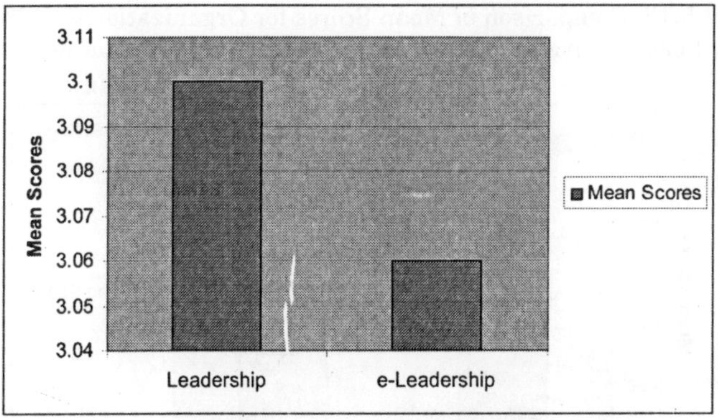

Chart 5.11: Comparison of Mean Scores for Trust under Leadership and E-Leadership in BPO and IT Sector as a Whole

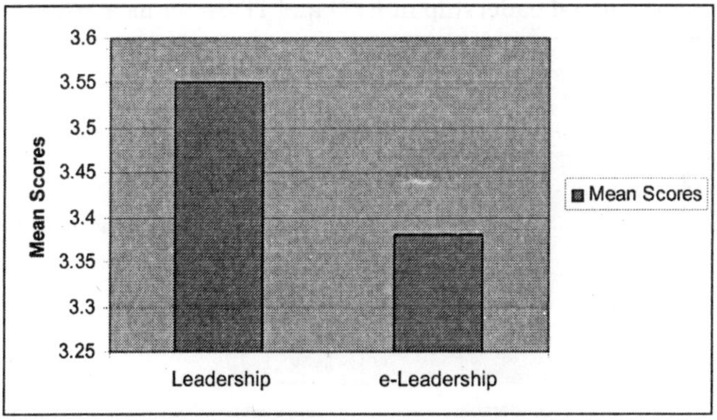

Chart 5.12: Comparison of Mean Scores for Commitment under Leadership and E-Leadership in BPO and IT Sector as a Whole

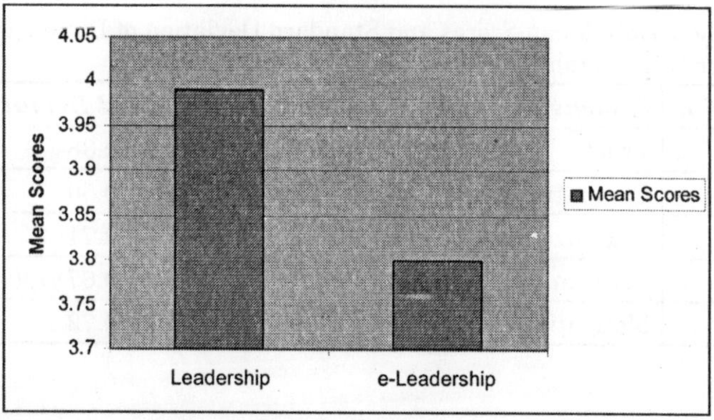

Chart 5.13: Comparison of Mean Scores for Organizational Culture under Leadership and E-Leadership in BPO and IT Sector as a Whole

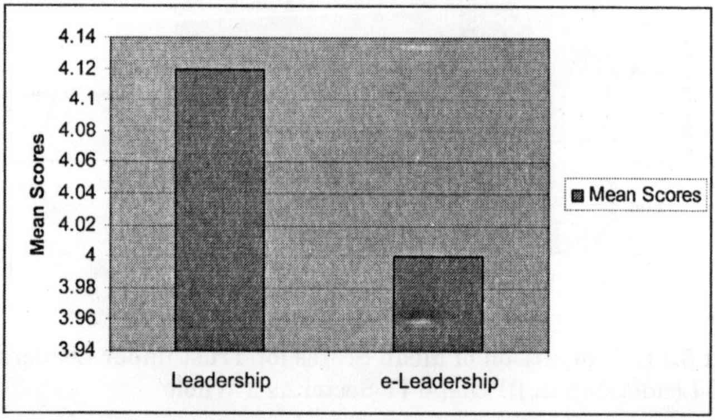

Chart 5.14: Comparison of Mean Scores for Performance under Leadership and E-Leadership in BPO and IT Sector as a Whole

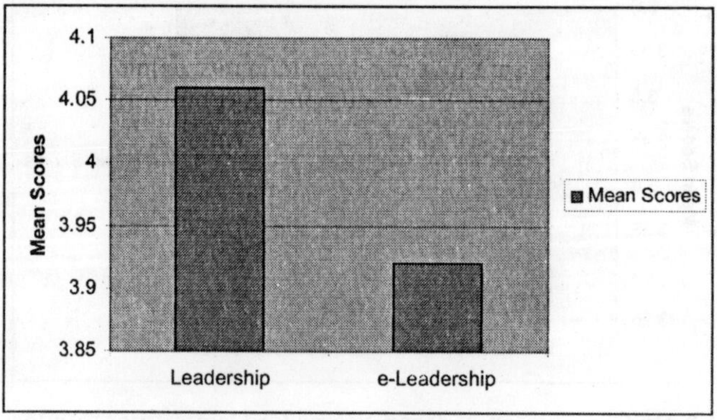

Chart 5.15: Comparison of Mean Scores for Performance under Leadership and E-Leadership in BPO and IT Sector as a Whole

5.2 Inferential Statistics

Since descriptive scores do not help us in drawing inferences about the significance of the mean scores and also the differences in the perceptions of leadership in BPO and IT sector, t-test has been carried out to find out the significant differences, if any, across the various dimensions in BPO and IT sector with respect to the perception of leadership.

5.2.1 BPO Sector

Table 5.2.1: Comparison between Different Dimensions under Leadership and E-Leadership for the BPO Sector

BPO Sector						
Sl. No.	*Variable*	*Mean (L)*	*Mean (EL)*	*S.D (L)*	*S.D (EL)*	*t-value*
1	Trust	3.06	3.02	0.24	0.35	0.90
2	Commitment	3.61	3.46	0.32	0.38	2.90*
3	Organizational Culture	4.06	3.99	0.45	0.52	0.96
4	Performance	4.11	4.05	0.45	0.56	-0.51
5	Motivation	4.07	4.06	0.49	0.58	0.16

**Significant at 0.01 level*

The comparison of the dimensions under leadership and e-leadership for the BPO sector shows that the two types of leadership i.e., traditional leadership and e-leadership are significantly different on the dimension of Commitment as depicted in Table 5.2.1. The mean value for Commitment in traditional leadership is 3.61 and for e-leadership are 3.46.

For the dimension of Commitment, the mean of traditional leadership is higher than that for e-leadership with a significant t-value. The scores clearly imply that traditional leadership has much impact on the commitment level of the team members as compared to the e-leadership.

Our hypothesis in the study states that there is a favourable bearing of e-leadership on commitment level in leader-follower dynamics as compared to traditional leadership. But the results show that traditional leadership has higher impact on Commitment as compared to e-leadership. Therefore, we can not accept Hypothesis 3 for BPO sector.

In BPO sector for other dimensions of leadership/ e-leadership t-value found is not significant. Hence, the Hypotheses 1, 2, 4 and 5 can not be accepted.

The comparison on the dimensions under leadership and e-leadership for the BPO sector shows that traditional leadership and e-leadership are significantly different on the dimension of Commitment. The scores clearly imply that traditional leadership has much impact on the commitment level of the employees as compared to the e-leadership. BPO is a sector where attrition rate is higher as compared to other sectors (ENS Economic Bureau, Feb. 2006), major reason being odd work schedules and monotony in the job. Situation gets worsened if the leader is also not physically present with the team members. Less interaction and the absence of non-verbal cues from the leader tend to make the employee to feel no kind of assurance from the organization side. This could result in less commitment to the organization from the employee side. Past studies have also supported the results that traditional leadership enhances the commitment level of the subordinates.

House (1977) proposed a theory of charismatic leadership that focused on how a leader can create an impression among subordinates that the leader has the competence and vision to achieve success. The result is an enthusiasm and commitment by subordinates to the group objectives.

Likewise, it has been shown that transformational leader gains a greater commitment from subordinates and induces them to transcend personal self-interest for the betterment of the group or organization not only with charisma but also by serving as a coach, teacher, or mentor (Bass, 1985; Yukl, 1989).

There are evidences present that transformational leaders enhance follower effort, satisfaction, commitment, and performance (Lowe, Kroeck, and Sivasubramaniam, 1996; Podsakoff, Mackenzie, Moorman, and Fetter, 1990; Yammarino, Spangler, and Bass, 1993).

Research of charismatic leadership has consistently found significant relationships with follower trust, effort, and commitment (Howell and Frost, 1989; Lowe et al., 1996).

In case of virtual situation, Staples (1997) has also reported that organizational commitment of their employees was one of the most important abiding concerns of managers of virtual workers. Research has also shown that the dispersion and dislocation characterizing virtual organizations may reduce communication among employees, increase their feelings of isolation, and consequently reduce their commitment to the organization (Huff, C., L. Sproull, and S. Kiesler, 1989).

No significant difference was found for the impact of traditional leadership and e-leadership on another variables viz. Trust, Motivation, Organizational Culture and Performance. As far as motivation level of the employees is concerned in BPO sector, it was understood during the personal interviews that there are various incentive and promotional schemes interconnected with the performance of the employees which keeps them motivated. Leader has not much role as he can not go beyond the available schemes to motivate a particular employee. Therefore, physical absence of the leader does not effect the motivation and performance of the employees to much extent in BPO sector. In such a competitive arena, the level of Trust among team members has certainly changed and does not get affected by the physical presence or absence of the leader as Trust is a psychological state at the individual level and develops through shared experiences, values and give and take.

5.2.2 IT Sector

Table 5.2.2: Comparison between Different Dimensions under Leadership and E-Leadership for the IT Sector

IT Sector						
Sl. No.	*Variable*	*Mean (L)*	*Mean (EL)*	*S.D (L)*	*S.D (EL)*	*t-value*
1	Trust	3.19	3.12	0.38	0.42	0.93
2	Commitment	3.36	3.27	0.53	0.61	0.77
3	Organizational Culture	3.77	3.53	0.37	0.65	2.28**
4	Performance	4.12	3.77	0.49	0.74	2.71*
5	Motivation	4.03	3.72	0.52	0.83	2.17**

**Significant at 0.01 level*
***Significant at 0.05 level*

As shown in Table 5.2.2, the comparison of the dimensions under Leadership and e-leadership for the IT sector shows that the two types of leadership i.e., traditional leadership and e-leadership are significantly different on the dimension of Organizational Culture, Performance and Motivation. The mean value for Organizational Culture in traditional leadership is 3.77 and for e-leadership is 3.53. The mean value is higher in case of traditional leadership as compared to e-leadership with a significant t-value.

Therefore, traditional leadership has much impact on the Organizational Culture as compared to the e-leadership. For the dimension of Performance, the mean value in traditional leadership is higher than that for e-leadership i.e., 4.12 and 3.77 respectively with a significant t-value. The scores clearly imply that traditional leadership has much impact on the performance level of the team members as compared to the situation in e-leadership. In case of Motivation also the mean score is 4.03 in traditional leadership situation which is higher than the mean score in e-leadership i.e., 3.72. Its t-value is also significant which shows that traditional leadership has more impact on motivation as compared to e-leadership. For other dimensions of leadership/e-leadership viz., Trust and Commitment, t-value is not significant.

Traditional leadership and e-leadership are found to be significantly different on the dimensions of Organizational Culture, Performance and Motivation when a comparison was done for the various dimensions of leadership and e-leadership for the IT sector.

According to the results of t-test it is clear that in IT sector e-leadership has negative impact on Organizational Culture, Motivation and Performance and no significant impact on Trust and Commitment as compared to traditional leadership. Subsequently, the hypotheses that e-leadership has positive impact on Organizational Culture, Motivation, Performance, Trust and Commitment, can not be accepted. Therefore, we reject Hypotheses 1, 2, 3, 4 and 5.

No significant difference was found between leadership and e-leadership in case of Commitment to the organization in IT sector. People get escalation once they shift from one organization to another because their experience is reckoned in a better way as compared to the parent organization. Subsequently, they are more likely to change the organization. This view point was explored during the personal interviews.

However, as far as Performance and Motivation level is concerned, traditional leadership definitely has an upper hand. The results are supported by several studies which have been carried out in past.

Bass (1985) and Yammarino and Bass (1990) showed that leaders high in transformational behaviours achieve maximum performance from followers because they are able to inspire followers to raise their criteria for success and develop innovative problem solving skills.

Bass (1985) also extended charismatic leadership to a theory of transformational leadership where the leader is able to inspire and activate subordinates to perform beyond expectations and to achieve goals beyond those normally set.

Tvorik and McGivern (1997) also showed that leadership is one of the most important areas that contribute to performance.

There are evidences that transformational leaders enhance follower effort, satisfaction, commitment, and performance (Lowe, Kroeck, & Sivasubramaniam, 1996; Podsakoff, Mac-Kenzie, Moorman, and Fetter, 1990; Yammarino, Spangler, and Bass, 1993).

Building on the work of Burns (1978), Bass (1985) defined transformational leadership and established a measurement instrument for the construct. From his perspective, transformational leaders motivate their followers to perform beyond normal expectations by transforming their thoughts and attitudes. They enlist their followers to buy into their vision and strive for its fulfillment. To accomplish this, transformational leaders exhibit the following kinds of behaviors: attributed charisma, inspirational motivation, intellectual stimulation, and individualized consideration (Bass and Avolio, 1994; Conger 1999).

Also studying transactional leadership, Hunt (1991) found that this type of leadership motivates followers by appealing to their self-interests (pay, status, rewards) because these are used in exchange for work.

5.2.3 BPO + IT Sector

Table 5.2.3: Comparison between Different Dimensions under Leadership and E-Leadership in the BPO and IT Sector as a Whole

BPO+IT Sector						
Sl. No	*Variable*	*Mean (L)*	*Mean (EL)*	*S.D (L)*	*S.D (EL)*	*t-value*
1	Trust	3.10	3.06	0.29	0.38	0.82
2	Commitment	3.55	3.38	0.40	0.50	3.19*
3	Organizational Culture	3.99	3.80	0.45	0.71	3.03*
4	Performance	4.12	4.00	0.46	0.67	1.85***
5	Motivation	4.06	3.92	0.50	0.71	2.01**

* *Significant at 0.01 level*
** *Significant at 0.05 level*
*** *Significant at 0.10 level*

The comparison of the dimensions under leadership and e-leadership for the BPO and IT sector taken together shows that the two types of leadership i.e., traditional leadership and e-leadership are significantly different on the dimension of Commitment, Organizational Culture, Performance and Motivation. The results have been shown in table 5.2.3. In case of Commitment the value of mean is 3.55 for traditional leadership and 3.38 for e-leadership. The mean value for Organizational Culture in traditional leadership is 3.99 and for e-leadership are 3.80. The mean value is higher in case of traditional leadership as compared to e-leadership with a significant t-value for both dimensions i.e., Commitment and Organizational Culture. Therefore, traditional leadership has much greater impact on the Organizational Culture and Commitment as compared to the e-leadership.

For the dimension of Performance, the mean value in traditional leadership is higher than that for e-leadership i.e., 4.12 and 4.00 respectively with a significant t-value.

The scores clearly imply that traditional leadership has a greater impact on the performance level of the team members as compared to the situation in e-leadership. In case of Motivation also the mean score is 4.06 in traditional leadership situation which is higher than the mean score in e-leadership i.e., 3.92. The t-value is also significant which shows that traditional leadership has greater impact on motivation as compared to e-leadership. For another dimension of leadership/e-leadership i.e., Trust, t-value is not significant.

When a comparison was done between different dimensions under leadership and e-leadership for the BPO and IT sector as a whole, it was revealed that Commitment level, Organizational Culture, Motivation level and Performance of the employees were high where traditional leadership was prevailing as compared to e-leadership. In case of Trust, no significant difference was found between leadership and e-leadership.

The above analysis clearly points out that hypotheses stated in the study do not hold true as e-leadership is not having a favorable impact on the various dimensions chosen for the study. The results show that traditional leadership has higher impact on Commitment, Organizational Culture, Motivation and Performance as compared to e-leadership. Therefore, we can not accept Hypotheses 1, 3, 4 and 5 for BPO and IT sector taken together. Since the t-value found is not significant for Trust, we can not accept the hypotheses 2.

Some of the studies carried out in recent past also support the result that an electronic interface is not a substitute for face-to-face communication (Abel, 1990; Sproull and Kiesler, 1991).

An exploratory investigation of the use of Web-based conferencing indicates that virtual and face-to-face teams had similar levels of communication effectiveness (Warkentin et al., 1997). However, a higher level of satisfaction was reported for face-to-face communication when compared to virtual teams in this exploratory study.

It has been suggested that Trust is temporal and fragile for groups with no face-to-face communication, which are culturally divided, or have no common past or plans for future collaboration, thus making CMC tools less effective (Jarvenpaa and Leidner, 1998, 1999; Jones and Bowie, 1998; Meyerson et al., 1996).

Understanding the relationship between technology and human behaviour is seen as critical for ensuring a higher level of user participation (Galegher and Kraut, 1992; Kelly et al., 2002; Wellman et al., 1996).

Systems failure due to the lack of understanding of social factors during the systems implementation phase has been documented in many research studies (Clark, 1996; Cornell and Balogna, 1992; Geisler and Rogers, 2000; Hirschheim, 1985; Olson et al., 1993; Orlikoski and Robey, 1990; Walsham and Han, 1991) and this is also applicable to the case of geographically dispersed collaboration (Hiltz and Turoff, 1978, 1992; Ludwig, 1999).

Several empirical studies on the Trust development process suggest that video and audio conferencing groups are nearly as good as face-to-face contact provided that participants engage in various getting-acquainted activities (e.g., text chat) over a network (Bos et al., 2002; Rocco, 1998; Zheng et al., 2002). However, the use of ICT such as video and audio for building trust is considered to represent slower progress towards full cooperation and is vulnerable to opportunistic behavior (Das and Teng, 1998).

In an empirical study, Fowler and Wackerbarth (1980) found that audio conferencing may be substituted for and can even outperform face-to-face meetings. However, face-to-face communication was found to be more effective than audio conferencing for tasks which rely on interpersonal communication and are more complex in nature (Fowler and Wackerbarth, 1980; Niederman and Beise, 1999).

Staples (1997) reported that organizational commitment of their employees was one of the most important abiding concerns of managers of virtual workers.

Research has also shown that the dispersion and dislocation characterizing virtual organizations may reduce communication among employees, increase their feelings of isolation, and consequently reduce their commitment to the organization (Huff, C., L. Sproull, and S. Kiesler, 1989).

Research of social psychologists have previously shown that computermediated intra-group communication is unable to support the fuller range of communicative acts typically employed by face-to-face groups (McKinlay, A., Procter, R., and Dunnet,1999; Spears, R., Lea, M. and Lee, S., 1990).

From the inferential analysis of the data it has been observed that on the dimension of Trust no significant difference is found between leadership and e-leadership (for BPO sector, IT sector and both sectors taken together). However, according to O' Connell's (1998) assessment of the impact of IT on human relationships and the system of interactions within the organization, "Trust will play a changed role in new environment. Trust develops with shared experience, values, and give-and-take that are the result of human communication. Satellites, electronic mail, and networks could reduce the dimensions of Trust to which we are accustomed. New dimensions of Trust may spring up in their place." This gives an idea that a whole new model of Trust is requisite which goes well with the new organizations i.e., the organizations which are empowered by the Information Technology.

From the present study it has also been observed that e-leadership has reduced the performance level of employees as compared to traditional leadership. It can be attributed to the fact that expectations of work performance may be machine driven. As we become accustomed to the speed and accuracy of the computer, we may expect employees to have the same qualities and produce in similar manner. Employees in some organizations will perceive this as dehumanizing and not congenial. Unions will take up the human environment as an issue. New ways of defining and using performance standards will be needed (O' Connell, 1998).

5.3 Correlational Analysis

After identifying the areas of significant differences in the mean scores of the various variables under leadership and e-leadership among different sectors, an attempt has been made to find out the degree of relationship among the different variables under study for leadership and e-leadership.

Pearson's Products-Moment correlations were computed in order to understand the relationship among the variables under leadership/e-leadership i.e., Trust, Commitment, Organization Culture, Performance and Motivation for BPO sector and IT sector taken together.

5.3.1 BPO + IT Sector - Leadership

Table 5.3.1 shows the relationship depicted statistically among the dimensions under leadership in BPO and IT sector as a whole.

Table 5.3.1: Coefficient of Correlations among the Dimensions under Leadership in BPO and IT Sector as a Whole

	TR	MOT	OC	PER	CM
TR	1.000				
MOT	.120	1.000			
OC	–.068	.787**	1.000		
PER	.066	.775**	.823**	1.000	
CM	–.006	.521**	.687**	.576**	1.000

***Correlation is significant at the 0.01 level (2-tailed).*

(I) Relationship of Trust with Other Variables

The correlational analysis for the variables under leadership in BPO and IT sector as a whole shows that Trust has no significant relationship with Commitment, Motivation, Organizational Culture and Performance.

(II) Relationship of Commitment with Other Variables

Commitment shows a highly significant and positive correlation with Motivation, Organizational Culture and Performance. The relationship between Commitment and Trust was not found to be significant.

(III) Relationship of Organizational Culture with Other Variables

In the case of Organizational Culture, a positive and highly significant correlation is found with Commitment, Performance and Motivation. No correlation is found between Trust and Organizational Culture.

(IV) Relationship of Performance with Other Variables

Performance shows an insignificant correlation with Trust. However, it shows a highly significant and positive relation with Commitment, Performance and Motivation.

(V) Relationship of Motivation with Other Variables

Motivation shows a positive and highly significant relation with Commitment, Organizational Culture, Performance and an insignificant relationship with Trust.

To summarize, we can say that in case of leadership in BPO and IT sector as a whole all variables have a positive and highly significant correlation among themselves except Trust which has an insignificant relationship with any of the other variable under study.

5.3.2 BPO + IT Sector: E-Leadership

Table 5.3.2 shows the statistical relationship among the dimensions under e-leadership in BPO and IT sector as a whole.

Table 5.3.2: Coefficient of Correlations among the Dimensions under E-Leadership in BPO and IT Sector as a Whole

	TR	**MOT**	**OC**	**PER**	**CM**
TR	1.000				
MOT	.536**	1.000			
OC	.512**	.793**	1.000		
PER	.478**	.852**	.855**	1.000	
CM	.481**	.660**	.783**	.716**	1.000

***Correlation is significant at the 0.01 level (2-tailed).*

(I) Relationship of Trust with Other Variables

The correlational analysis for the variables under e-leadership in BPO and IT sector as a whole shows that Trust has positive and significant relationship with Commitment, Motivation, Organizational Culture and Performance.

(II) Relationship of Commitment with Other Variables

Commitment shows a highly significant and positive correlation with Trust, Motivation, Organizational Culture and Performance.

(III) Relationship of Organizational Culture with Other Variables

In the case of Organizational Culture, a positive and highly significant correlation is found with Trust, Commitment, Performance and Motivation.

(IV) Relationship of Performance with Other Variables

Performance shows highly significant and positive correlation with Trust, Commitment, Performance and Moti-vation.

(V) Relationship of Motivation with Other Variables

Motivation shows a positive and highly significant relation with Commitment, Organizational Culture, Performance and Trust.

To summarize, we can say that in case of e-leadership in BPO and IT sector as a whole all variables have a positive and highly significant correlation among themselves.

In an attempt to find out the degree of relationship among different variables under study for leadership and e-leadership, it was found that in case of leadership all variables viz., Commitment, Organizational Culture, Motivation and Performance have a positive and highly significant correlation among themselves while Trust has an insignificant relationship with any of the other variable under study in leadership. In case of e-leadership all variables viz., Trust, Commitment, Organizational Culture, Motivation and Performance have a positive and highly significant correlation among themselves.

The trend which has come forward from the correlation analysis of the various variables indicates that a cluster of Motivation, Organizational Culture, Commitment and Performance emerges with highly significant correlation among themselves in leadership as well as e-leadership.

Much popular and scholarly attention has also been focused on the hypothesis that strong cultures defined as "a set of norms and values that are widely shared and strongly held throughout the organization" (O'Reilly and Chatman, 1996), enhance firm's performance. This hypothesis is based on the intuitively powerful idea that organizations benefit from having highly motivated employees dedicated to common goals (Peters and Waterman, 1982; Deal and Kennedy, 1982; Kotter and Heskett, 1992).

Strong cultures can enhance employees' motivation and performance because they perceive that their actions are freely chosen (O'Reilly, 1989; O'Reilly and Chatman, 1996).

According to Smircich (1983), culture conveys to employees a sense of identity, facilitates the generation of commitment to something larger than the self, and enhances social system stability, as well as guiding and shaping behaviour.

Studies have found strong positive relationships between organizational commitment and desirable work outcomes such as performance, adaptability, and job satisfaction (Angle and Perry, 1981; Hunt et al., 1985; Mowday et al., 1974; Porter et al., 1974; Steers, 1977).

5.4 Multiple Regression Analysis

To gain an insight into the relationships among various variables under leadership/e-leadership further and to identify the predictive relationships between the two sets of variables, if any, multiple regression analysis was performed.

From the correlational tables it can be seen that there are significant linear correlations among various dimensions i.e., Trust, Commitment, Organizational Culture, Performance and Motivation. In order to see multiple interactions between different variables in predicting certain outcome variables Multiple Regression Analysis was performed on the data. The findings helped in identifying the most potent predictors, their hierarchical order, individual positive and negative contributions and the Multiple R.

The stepwise regression analysis focused on picking up the best set of predictor variables in determining the statistical significance of their prediction of criteria. Using different dimensions under leadership/e-leadership and outcome variables as criteria, stepwise method of regression analysis was applied to the independent variables under study.

The equation turned out to be the best when 'F' value became intolerant, and predicted the dependent variable and outcome variables dimension to the nearest correct values. Stepwise multiple regression is:

$y = a + b_1 x_1 + b_2 x_2 + b_3 x_3 \ldots\ldots. b_n x_n$

When' y' is the dependent variable

'x_1', 'x_2', 'x_3' .... 'x_n' are independent variables

'b_1', 'b_2' .... 'b_n' are the regression coefficient

'a' is the constant.

An attempt was made to predict 'Organizational Culture' for leadership and e-leadership in BPO sector and IT sector taken together. There is a set of equations in which Organizational Culture was assumed as the dependent variable and other four variables as independent variables viz., Trust, Commitment, Performance and Motivation. The stepwise multiple regression analysis was performed.

The results are entered in the tables as follows:

Table 5.9a: displays the results for Organizational Culture for leadership.

Table 5.9b: displays the results for Organizational Culture for e-leadership.

5.4.1 Prediction of Organizational Culture

Organizational Culture is the workplace environment formulated from the interaction of the employees in the workplace. Organizational culture is defined by all of the life experiences, strengths, weaknesses, education, upbringing, and so forth of the employees. While executive leaders play a large role in defining organizational culture by their actions and leadership, all employees contribute to the organizational culture.

Organizational Culture is a multidimensional and multifaceted construct. The Organizational Culture in an organization reflects the totality of the organization. Perhaps most importantly, Culture penetrates to the essence of an organization. It is almost analogous with the concept of personality in relation to the individual and this acute sense of what an organization is – its mission, core values – seems to have become a necessary asset of the modern company. Organizational Culture evolves over a period of time as a joint function of internal and external factors. As a result of this evolutionary nature of Organizational Culture, each organization develops a unique culture, although part of it may be shown by a number of organizations. There is no universal set of dimensions or properties for Organizational Culture. Although Organizational Culture is shaped by a variety of organizational factors, culture itself impacts both individual and group performance. Organizational Culture refers to the relatively enduring set of values and norms that underline a social system. More or less it taps several dimensions of the organization. In the present study, Organizational Culture was taken as dependent variable and the other four variables were taken as independent variables so as to find out the contribution of these independent variables in the prediction of Organizational Culture.

(A) Organizational Culture for Leadership

Dependent Variable: Organizational Culture

Table 5.4.1a: Predicting 'Organizational Culture' for Traditional Leadership (n= 204)

Sl. No.	*Independent Variables*	*r between IV & DV*	*R value*	R^2	*β Value*	*p*
1.	PR	0.823**	.823	.677	0.82	.000

2.	PR+CM	0.687**	.863	.744	0.32	.000
3.	PR+CM+ MOT	0.787**	.886	.785	0.32	.000
4.	PR+CM+ MOT+TR	−0.068	.896	.802	-0.14	.000

*** significant at 0.01 level*

As presented in Table 5.4.1a, the results indicate that when independent variables were entered in the regression model with Organizational Culture for the Leadership, Performance contributed to approximately 68% of the variance, with beta weights to be 0.82 (which indicates the magnitude of the variables contribution to explain variance). An increase of 7% was observed when Commitment entered in the equation with β value being 0.32. Consequently other independent variables viz. Motivation and Trust entered in the equation accounted for 80% of the variance with β values being 0.32 and –0.14 respectively. A negative beta value of Trust shows that it contributed in a negative manner.

Some of the early studies like Siehl and Martin (1990) have also reported mixed evidence of a positive relationship between Culture and Performance.

Motivation was also found to be a predictor of Organizational Culture. In earlier studies also it was found that Culture can enhance employees' Motivation and Performance because they perceive that their actions are freely chosen. This relationship between Organizational Culture and Motivation was found by O'Reilly (1989) and O'Reilly and Chatman (1996).

In the present context, Commitment also contributed in the prediction of Organizational Culture. Likewise, Smircich (1983) suggested the relation between Organizational Culture and Commitment. He shows that culture conveys to employees a sense of identity, facilitates the generation of commitment to something larger than the self, and enhances social system stability, as well as guiding and shaping behaviour.

Though Trust entered in the equation but contributed in a negative manner to the prediction of Organizational Culture, thereby implying that as it has a negative correlation with Organizational Culture in the current context.

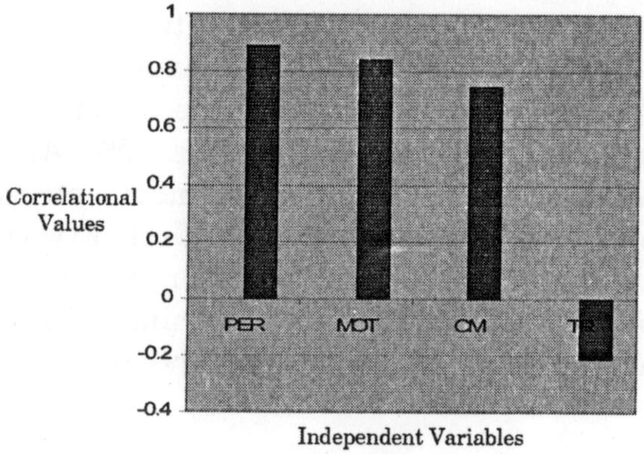

Chart 6.1: Correlation between Organizational Culture and Indepentdent Variables

Key to Abbreviations

PER - Performance

MOT - Motivation

CM - Commitment

TR - Trust

(B) Organizational Culture for E-Leadership

Dependent Variable: Organizational Culture

Table 5.4.1b: Predicting 'Organizational Culture' for E-Leadership (n= 96)

S. No	*Independent Variables*	*r between IV & DV*	*R value*	R^2	β *Value*	*p*
1.	PR	0.855**	.855	.731	0.856	.000
2.	PR+CM	0.783**	.890	.791	0.35	.000

*** significant at 0.01 level*

When regression was run to predict organizational culture for e-leadership, it was found that among four independent variables only two variables, namely Performance and Commitment entered into the equation. The results are shown in Table 5.4.1b. It indicates that Performance contributed 73% of the variance with beta weights to be 0.86 (which indicates the magnitude of the variables contribution to explained variance). When Commitment entered into the equation the total contribution of the variance became 79%. An increase of 6% was observed when Commitment entered in the equation with β value being 0.35. The other two variables i.e, Motivation and Trust did not enter into the regression equation and thereby contributed nothing to the prediction of Organizational Culture in e-leadership.

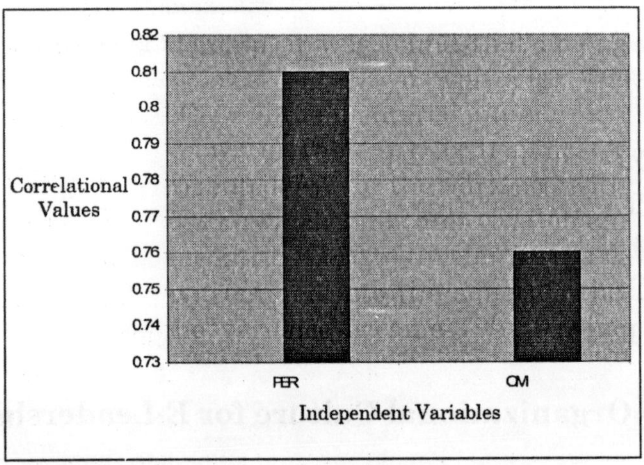

Chart 6.2: Correlations between Organizational Cultue and Independent Variables

Key to Abbreviations

PER - Performance

CM - Commitment

6 SUMMARY AND CONCLUSIONS

6.1 Summary and Conclusions of the Study

The present study was conducted to understand the impact of Information Technology on the process of leadership of selected organizations with a focus on Business Process Outsourcing (BPO) and IT industry. Leadership and E-leadership in the organizations was studied with an emphasis on Organizational Culture, Trust, Commitment, Motivation and Performance of the employees. For the purpose of the present study, five companies in the BPO industry and three companies in the IT sector were selected. This chapter presents a brief summary of the study including the review of its major findings.

In the present research, the physical absence/presence of the leader on the overall sample of BPO and IT industry as well as for the individual sector was examined against five dependent variables viz. Organizational Culture, Trust, Commitment, Motivation and Performance. An inter company comparison of the work culture was done. A set of objectives and hypotheses were formulated for this purpose.

The study was based on non-probability incidental sampling. The total sample consisted of 300 respondents out of which 204 were from BPO Industry and 96 from IT Industry. The data was collected using both questionnaire and semi-structured interview methods of data collection.

The variables identified and studied for the purpose of the present study are stated below.

(a) **Demographic variables** – Age, sex, education, salary and experience.

(b) **Trust** - For the purpose of identifying the trust level among team members, an acquired Trust scale developed by Jack R. Gibb (1972) was used.

(c) **Commitment** – It was studied using a scale developed by Buchanan (1974) measuring:

- Job Identification
- Job Involvement
- Organizational Loyalty

(d) **Organizational Culture** – It was measured by using the Organizational Climate Questionnaire (OCQ) by Adrian Furnham and Leonard D. Goodstein, 1997 assessing organization in six different areas namely:

- Role Clarity
- Communication
- Reward System
- Career Development
- Innovation
- Teamwork and Support

(e) **Performance** – The scale by Pam Jones and Joy Palmer (1996) was used to measure Performance. The representation of different components is given below:

- Purpose
- Performance
- Learning

(f) **Motivation** – To measure the motivation level, a scale of 9 items as developed by M. S. Shookla (2004) was used.

The data thus obtained was tabulated and subjected to statistical analysis namely correlation, stepwise multiple regression analysis and t-test. Another set of qualitative data was obtained with the help of semi-structured interviews.

The analysis of data was carried out for both sectors independently as well as a whole to obtain insight into the impact of e-leader in the organizations.

The results from the Descriptive and Correlational Analysis of the dimensions of Leadership in BPO and IT Sector as a whole show that:

(a) Performance under traditional leadership in BPO sector has the highest mean score while trust has least mean score with least standard deviation.

(b) Motivation under e-leadership in BPO sector has the highest mean score with highest standard deviation while trust has least mean score with least standard deviation.

(c) Performance under traditional leadership in IT sector has the highest mean score while trust has least mean score. Commitment shows the highest standard deviation and Organizational Culture shows lowest standard deviation.

(d) Performance under e-leadership in IT sector has the highest mean score while trust has lowest mean value. The highest and lowest standard deviation is shown by Motivation and Trust respectively.

(e) Performance under traditional leadership in BPO and IT sector has the highest mean score as well standard deviation while trust has least mean score as well standard deviation.

(f) Performance under e-leadership in BPO and IT sector has the highest mean score while trust has lowest mean value. The highest and lowest standard deviation is shown by Motivation and Trust respectively.

(g) In case of leadership in BPO and IT sector as a whole, all variables i.e., Commitment, Organizational Culture, Motivation and Performance have a positive and highly significant correlation among themselves except Trust which has no significant relationship with any other variable under study.

(h) In case of e-leadership in BPO and IT sector as a whole, all variables have a positive and highly significant correlation among themselves.

The results of the Inferential Analysis to measure the differences among the variables under leadership and e-leadership across different sectors show that:

1. Traditional leadership and e-leadership are significantly different on the dimension of commitment in the BPO sector.
2. No significant difference was found on the dimensions of Trust, Organizational Culture, Motivation and Performance between leadership and e-leadership in BPO sector.
3. In IT sector, a significant difference was found on the dimensions of Organizational Culture, Motivation and Performance between leadership and e-leadership.
4. No significant difference was found between leadership and e-leadership on the dimensions of Trust and Commitment.
5. When BPO and IT sector were taken as a whole, a significant difference between leadership and e-leadership was found for Commitment, Organizational Culture, Motivation and Performance.

The results from the Regression Analysis for the prediction of Organizational Culture taken under study for leadership and e-leadership show that:

(a) For predicting Organizational Culture for the leadership, Performance, Motivation and Commitment explained the variance with Trust, thus contributing negatively to Organizational Culture.

(b) Performance and Commitment contributed significantly in predicting Organizational Culture for e-leadership.

The findings of the study have been discussed in the light of the similar studies done in the area and the existing literature available. The quantitative findings were further substantiated with the data obtained through semi-structured interviews.

6.2 Relevance of the Study

The present study, to a certain extent, highlights the importance of the feel and presence of human touch in the work place. No research work, however, is complete to its fullest extent – it's an ongoing process. The importance and utility of this small effort lies in its practicality and if this work is able to stimulate further research in this area, it would achieve its purpose.

The implications or practical applications of any research must necessarily be sought in the extent to which it is applicable in actual life set-up. The quantitative and the qualitative findings and the discussions following them have been detailed earlier. Here, the significance and the practical applications of these findings have been considered. Owing to rich data-base and intricate results, the findings of theoretical importance are so numerous that dealing with each of them once again here would amount to a voluminous repetition of the facts and their relevance that have already been enunciated at appropriate places in the discussion section.

In any organization, the importance of leader can never be underestimated and overlooked. In the present study, a modest effort has been made to study the effect of Information Technology on the phenomenon of leadership. An exploratory study of the BPO and IT industry has been carried out by studying five different BPO and three IT companies. Each company has been found to be having its own distinct work culture influencing identification, involvement and loyalty of the employees towards their job and the organization. Each company provides a particular type of set-up by virtue of the nature of job, rules, regulations, recognition, the compensation which affect and in-turn get influenced by the people who come from different backgrounds and with different set of individual work values which may help or hinder the development of a functional and viable work culture.

The present study has shown that if organizations do not make attempts to understand the importance of human touch, to develop relation between the leaders and the team members, the absence of leader from the work place may have detrimental impact on human dynamics. The major implication of this study can be viewed in the light of the companies and the major variables being studied in the work have been shown to be negatively influenced by the absence of the leader.

Earlier in the study we had raised the issue as is true that we are using advanced information technology to lead and to follow without necessarily knowing the full extent of its impact on human dynamics in organizations. Is it really working? The relevance of the study lies in the fact that it tries to identify the manner in which e-leadership is contributing to the business organizations: positive or negative. Findings show that there are certain variables related to leader follower relationship in the business organizations which need much more attention in e-leadership scenario as compared to traditional leadership. Some of the variables where the consideration is required in e-leadership situation on the part of the organizations have been identified in the present study namely Motivation, Trust, Commitment, Organizational Culture, and Performance as e-leadership is having a downbeat effect on these variables as compared to traditional leadership.

To summarize, it was found that Commitment, Organizational Culture, Motivation and Performance were high where traditional leadership was prevailing as compared to e-leadership. In case of Trust, no significant difference was found between leadership and e-leadership.

Hence, the hypotheses stated earlier i.e., Hypotheses 1, 2, 3, 4 and 5 in the study are rejected.

6.3 Suggestions for Further Research

The topic of present investigation has significant relevance for understanding the physical absence of the leader in an organization i.e. the e-leadership. The following refinements and extension of the present problems may thus be undertaken.

1. Leader's View Point

The leaders of the teams under study could be included as part of the sample. This could provide a better and exhaustive picture of e-leadership.

2. More Variables

More variables along with the intervening variables can be taken as the dimension of leadership/e-leadership to understand the impact of absence in a better way.

3. More Sectors

The study can be further extended to more such sectors where the concept of e-leadership is prevailing.

4. Impact of Various IT Tools

The impact of various IT mediated tools like Audio and video can be studied separately.

5. Study of Virtual Teams

Apart from virtual leaders, virtual teams can also be studied as an extension of the study.

6. Management View Point

The concept of e-leadership could be studied from the point of view of management.

7. Different Regions

The study may give a broader picture if companies from different regions in the country are considered, for it may bring different aspects pertaining to the location of the organizations as well.

6.4 Limitations of the Study

As limitations are inherent in all research investigations, it is important that these be brought to light. Some of the limitations of the present study may be enumerated as follows:

E-leadership is relatively a new and evolving concept and only a limited number of resources are available that can be studied in detail. There are several arguments about the definition and the role of the e-leader that remains unresolved. The study was confined to Delhi and NCR and only five companies in the BPO industry and three companies in the IT sector were taken for the purpose of the study.

Since e-leadership is a new topic, several books and articles on the subject were still under publication at the time when the present work was carried out. Hence, the same could not be incorporated. Assessment of the impact of physical absence of leader has been done from the perspective of team members only. By studying the perspective of leaders also, one could have gained a broader insight.

The generalizations occurring from this study are more conducive and are based on the perceptions of a limited to a particular group of employees who were included. In other words, the limitation comes from the sampling technique used, which is non-probability incidental sampling. The major inherent drawback of this technique is that it does not provide the researcher with any kind of sound foundation for making general inferences about the population from which the sample is drawn. These limitations can be duly considered by future researches in this area.

BIBLIOGRAPHY

- Abel, M. J. (1990) 'Experiences in an exploratory distributed organization', in Galegher, J., Kraut, R., and Agate, C. (eds), Intellectual Team Work: Social and Technological Foundations of Cooperative Work (pp. 489-510). Hillside, NJ: Lawrence Erlbaum.
- Allen, Michael P., Panian, S.K., and Lotz, Roy E. (1979) 'Managerial succession and organizational performance: a recaicitrant problem revisited', Administrative Science Quarterly, 21, 167-180.
- Amarchand, D., and Jayraj, B.J. (1992) 'Organization culture and effectiveness', Global Business Press, New Delhi.
- Andaleeb, Syed S. (1992) 'The trust concept: research issues for channels of distribution', Research in Marketing, 11, 1-34.
- Anderson, E., and Weitz, B. (1989) 'Determinants of continuity in conventional industrial channel dyads', Marketing Science, 8(4), 310.
- Angle, H. L., and Perry, J. L. (1981) 'An empirical assessment of organizational commitment and organizational effectiveness', Administrative Science Quarterly, 2(6), 1-14.

- Angle, H.L, Perry, J.L. (1983) 'Organizational commitment–individual and organizational influence', Work and Occupation, 10, 123-146.
- Annunzio, S. (2001) E-Leadership: Proven Techniques for Creating an Environment of Speed and Flexibility in the Digital Economy, Simon and Schuster NY.
- Aryee, S., Wyatt, T. and Min, M.K. (1991) 'Antecedents of organizational commitment and turnover intentions among professional accountants in different employment settings in Singapore', The Journal of Social Psychology, 131 (4), 545-556.
- Avolio, B.J. (1999) Full Leadership Development: Building the Vital Forces in Organizations, Thousand Oaks, CA: Sage.
- Avolio, B.J. and Kahai, S. (2003) 'Adding the "e" to e-leadership: how it may impact your leadership', Organizational Dynamics, 31(4), 325-338.
- Avolio, B. J., Kahai, S., and Dodge, G. E. (2001) 'E-leadership: implications for theory, research and practice', Leadership Quarterly, 11(4), 615-668.
- Axelrod, R. (1984) The Evolution of Cooperation, Basic Books.
- Barber, Bernard (1983) The Logic and Limits of Trust, New Brunswick, NJ: Rutgers University Press.
- Bass, B.M. (1985) Leadership and Performance Beyond Expectations, New York: Free Press.
- Bass, B.M., and Avolio, B.J. (1994) Improving Organizational Effectiveness Through Transformational Leadership, Thousand Oaks, CA: Sage.
- Becker, H.S. (1960) 'Notes on the concept of commitment', American Journal of Sociology, 66, 32-42.
- Bennis, W., and Nanus, B. (1985) Leaders: The Strategies for Taking Charge, NY: Harper and Row.

- Bennis, W.G. (1959) Leadership theory and administrative behaviour: the problem of authority, Administrative Science Quarterly, 4, 259-260.
- Blades, J. W. (1986) Rules for Leadership, National Defense University Press, Washington, DC.
- Blake, Robert, R. and Mouton, Jane, S. (1985) The Managerial Grid: The Key to Leadership Excellence, Houston: Gulf Publishing Co.
- Blau, P. (1964) Human Capital, Columbia University Press: New York.
- Bock, R. D. (1975) Multivariate Statistical Methods in Behavioral Research, Mc Graw-Hill, New York.
- Bos, N., Olson, J., Gergle, D., Olson, G., and Wright, Z. (2002) 'Effects of four computer-mediated communications channels on trust development', Proceedings of the SIGCHI Conference on Human Factors in Computing Systems, 135-140.
- Buchanan, B. (1974) 'Building organizational commitment: The socialization of managers in work organizations', Administrative Science Quarterly, 19, 533–546.
- Buchanan, D., and Huczynski, A. (1997) Organisational Behaviour: An Introductory Text, Prentice Hall, London.
- Buford, J. A., Jr., Bedeian, A. G., and Lindner, J.R. (1995) Management in Extension (3rd ed.), Columbus, Ohio: Ohio State University Extension.
- Burns, James MacGregor (1978) Leadership, NY: Harper and Row, Publishers.
- Butler, J. K. (1991) 'Towards understanding and measuring conditions of trust: evolution of a condition of trust inventory', Journal of Management, 17, 643-663.

- Bycio, P., Hackett, R.D., Allen, J. S (1995) 'Further assessment of Bass' (1985) conceptualization of transactional and transformational leadership', Journal of Applied Psychology, 80, 469-468.
- Campbell, J.P. (1970) Managerial Behavior, Performance, and Effectiveness, New York: McGraw-Hill.
- Cantor, N., and Mischel, W. (1979) 'Prototypes of person perception', in Berkowitz, E.L. (eds.), Advances in Experimental Social Psychology, 12, 3-52. New York: Academic.
- Clark, H.H. (1996) Using Language, Cambridge, MA: Cambridge University Press.
- Collins, J.C. and Porras, J. I. (1994) Built to Last, HarperCollins, New York, NY.
- Collins, J.C., and Porras, J.I. (1989) 'Purpose, mission, and vision', in Ray, M., and Rinzler, A. (eds.) The New Paradigm in Business: Emerging Strategies for Leadership and Organizational Change by the World Business Academy, 1993, 82-89, New York: Jeremy P. Tarcher.
- Conger, J.A. (1998) 'Qualitative research as the cornerstone methodology for understanding leadership', Leadership Quarterly, 9, 107-121.
- Conger, J.A. (1999) 'Charismatic and transformational leadership in organizations: an insider's perspective on these developing streams of research.' Leadership Quarterly, 10, 145-179.
- Conger, J.A., and Kanungo, R.N. (1998) Charismatic Leadership in Organizations, Thousand Oaks, CA.: Sage.
- Conger, J.A., Kanungo, R.N. (1987) 'Toward a behavioural theory of charismatic leadership in organizational settings', Academy of Management Review, 12, 637-647.

- Connell, J., Ferres, N., and Travaglione, A. (2002) 'Engendering trust in the workplace: the importance of perceived organizational support', Manuscript submitted for publication.
- Cornell, P., and Balogna, M. (1992) 'Work evolution and the new office', Proceedings of the Workshop on Productivity in the Knowledge Intensive Organization.
- Darcy, T., Kleiner, B.H. (1991) 'Leadership for change in a turbulent environment', Leadership and Organization Development Journal, 12, 12–16.
- Darling, R. John and T.M. Box, (1999) 'Keys to success in the leadership of multinational corporations, 1990 through 1997, S.A.M. Advanced Management Journal, autumn, 16-20.
- Das, T.K., and Bing-Sheng Teng (1998) 'Between trust and control: developing confidence in partner cooperation in alliances', Academy of Management Review, 23(3), 491-512.
- Dasgupta, P. (1988) 'Trust as a commodity', in Gambetta, D.G. (eds.), Trust, 49-72, New York: Basil Blackwell.
- Deal, T., and Kennedy, A. (1999) The New Corporate Cultures: Revitalizing the Workplace After Downsizing, Mergers and Reengineering, London: Orion Business Books.
- Denison, Daniel R. (1990) Corporate Culture and Organizational Effectiveness, New York: John Wiley and Sons.
- Deutsch, M. (1960) 'The effect of motivational orientation upon trust and suspicion', Human Relations, 13, 123-140.
- Drucker, P. F. (1993) Post-Capitalist Society, New York: Harper Business.

- Dubin, R. (1970) Human Relations in Administration, New Delhi, Prentice Hall of India.
- Dubin, Robert. (1959) 'Deviant behavior and social structure: continuities in social theory', American Sociological Review, 24, 147-163.
- Dwyer, F. Robert, Paul, H. Schurr, and Sejo, Oh (1987) 'Developing buyer-seller relationships,' Journal of Marketing, 51: April, 11-27.
- Eisenhardt, K. M. (1989) 'Making fast decisions in high-velocity environments', Academy of Management Journal, 32, 543-576.
- Eisenhardt, Kathleen M. (1989) "Agency theory: an assessment and review," Academy of Management Review, 14(1), 57-74.
- Eitzen, Stanley, D., and Norman, Yetman, R. (1972) "Managerial change longevity and organizational effectiveness', Administrative Science Quarterly, 17, 110-116.
- Farson, Richard and Crichton, Michael (1996) Management of the Absurd, New York: Simon and Schuster.
- Feldman, J. M. (1981) 'Beyond attribution theory: cognitive processes in performance appraisal', Journal of Applied Psychology, 66, 127-148.
- Feldman, J. M. (1986) 'A note on the statistical correction of halo error', Journal of Applied Psychology, 71, 173-176.
- Fiedler, F. E., Garcia, J. E. (1987) New Approaches to Effective Leadership: Cognitive Resources and Organizational Performance, Wiley, New York, NY.
- Fiedler, Fred E. (1996) 'Research on leadership selection and training: one view of the future,' Administrative Science Quarterly, 41, 241-250.
- Fowler, G. D., and Wackerbarth, M. E. (1980) 'Audio teleconferencing versus face-to-face conferencing: a

synthesis of the literature', Western Journal of Speech Communication, 44, summer, 236-252.

- Furnham, A., and Goodstein, L. (1997) The Organizational Climate Questionnaire, The 1997 Annual Consulting, Pfeiffer and Company.
- Galegher, J., and Kraut, R. E. (1992) 'Computer-mediated communication and collaborative writing: media influence and adaptation to communication constraints', Proceedings of the Conference on Computer Supported Cooperative Work, 155-162.
- Gambetta, D. (1988) Trust: Making and Breaking Cooperative Relations, Blackwell: New York 1988.
- Gamson, William, A., and Scotch, Norman, A. (1964) 'Scapegoating n baseball', American Journal of Sociology, 70, 69-72.
- Gardner, John W. (1990) On Leadership, New York: Free Press.
- Geisler, C., and Rogers, E. H. (2000) 'Technological mediation for design collaboration', Proceedings of IEEE Professional Communication Society International Professional Communication Conference and Proceedings of the 18th Annual ACM International Conference on Computer Documentation: Technology and Teamwork, 395-405.
- Gibb, Tori, J. R. (1972) 'Theory and practice', in Pfeiffer, J. W., and Jones, J. E. (eds.), The 1972 Annual Handbook for Group Facilitators, La Jolla, Calif: University Associates.
- Gilbert, T. (1998) A Leisurely Look at Worthy Performance: The 1998 ASTD Training and Performance Yearbook, Woods, J., and Gortada, J. (eds), New York: McGraw-Hill.
- Good, D. (1988) 'Individuals, interpersonal relations, and trust', in Gambetta, D.G. (eds.) Trust, 31-48, New York: Basil Blackwell.

- Graen, G.B., Uhl-Bien, M. (1995) 'Relationship-based approach to leadership: development of leader-member exchange LMX theory', Leadership Quarterly, 6, 219-247.
- Grusky, O. (1963) 'Managerial succession and organizational effectiveness', American Journal of Sociology, 69, 21-31.
- Gulati, R. (1995) 'Does familiarity breed trust? the implications of repeated ties for contractual choice in alliances', Academy of Management Journal, 38, 85-112.
- Hagberg, Richard, and Heifetz, J. (1998) 'Corporate Culture/ Organization Culture: Understanding and Assesment', http://www.hegnet.com.
- Hall, D. T., Schneider, B., and Nygren, H. T. (1970) 'Personal factors in organizational identification', Administrative Science Quarterly, 15, 179-190.
- Hall, Richard H. (1977) Organizations: Structure and Process, 2nd edition, Englewood Cliffs, NJ: Prentice-Hall.
- Hambrick, Donald C., and Mason, Phyllis A. (1984) 'Upper echelons: the organization as a reflection of its top managers.' Academy of Management Review, 9, 193-206.
- Hennessey, J. T. (1998) 'Reinventing government: does leadership make the difference?', Public Administration Review, 58(6), 522–32.
- Herzberg, E. (1966) Work and the Nature of Man, Cleveland: World Publishing Company.
- Herzberg, F., Mausner, B., and Snyderman, B. B. (1959) The Motivation to Work, New York: John Wiley and Sons.
- Hiltz, S. R. and Turoff, M. (1993) The Network Nation, Revised Edition, Cambridge, MA: MIT Press.
- Hiltz, S. R., and Turoff, M. (1978) The Network Nation:

Human Communication Via Computer, London: Addison-Wesley.

- Hiltz, S. R., and Turoff, M. (1992) 'Virtual meetings: computer conferencing and distributed group support,' in Bostrom, R.P., Waston, R.T., and Kinney, S. (eds.), Computer Augmented Teamwork, 67-85, New York: Van Nostrand Reinhold.
- Hiltz, S.R., Turoff, M. (1992) 'Structuring computer-mediated communication systems to avoid information overload', CACM, 28(7), 682-689, July 1985, reprinted in Marca, D., and Bock, G. (eds.), Groupware: Software for Computer-Supported Cooperative Work, Washington DC, IEEE Computer Society Press.
- Hirschheim, R. (1985) Office Automation: A Social and Organizational Perspective, Chichester, UK: John Wiley.
- Hosmer, L. (1995) 'Trust: the connecting link between organizational theory and philosophical ethics', Academy of Management Review, 20, 379-403.
- House, R. J., and Aditya, R. N. (1997) 'The social scientific study of leadership: quo vadis?', Journal of Management, 23, 409-473.
- House, R.J., Mitchell, T.R. (1974) 'Path-goal theory and leadership', Journal of Contemporary Business, 3, 79-81.
- Howell, J.M. (1986) 'Charismatic leadership: effects of leadership style and group productivity on individual adjustment and performance', Dissertation Abstracts International, 48.
- Howell, J.M., and Avolio, B.J. (1992) 'The ethics of charismatic leadership: submission or liberation?', Academy of Management Executive, 6, 2, 43-54.
- Howell, J.M., and Frost, P.J. (1989) 'A laboratory study of charismatic leadership', Organizational Behavior and Human Decision Process, 43, 243-269.

- Hrebiniak, L.G., and Alutto, J.A. (1972) 'Personal and role-related factors in the development of organizational commitment,' Administrative Science Quarterly, 17, 555–573.
- Huff, C., Sproull, L., and Kiesler, S. (1989) 'Computer communication and organizational commitment: tracing the relationship in a city government', Journal of Applied Social Psychology, 19, 1371-1391.
- Hunt, J.G. (1991) Leadership: A New Synthesis, Newbury Park, CA: Sage Publications.
- Hunt, S.D., Chonko, L., Wood, V.R. (1985) 'Organizational commitment and marketing', Journal of Marketing, 49, 112-126.
- Jarvenpaa, S.L., and Leidner, D.E. (1998) 'Communication and trust in global virtual teams,' Journal of Computer Mediated Communication, 3(4), 1-36.
- Jarvenpaa, S. L., and Leidner, D. E. (1999) 'Communication and trust in global virtual teams,' Organization Science, 10, 791-815.
- Jarvenpaa, S., Knoll, K., and Leidner, D. (1998) 'Is anybody out there? antecedents of trust in global virtual teams,' Journal of Management Information Systems, 14, 29-64.
- Jensen, Michael C., and Meckling, William, H. (1976) 'Theory of the firm: Managerial behavior, agency costs and ownership structure,' Journal of Financial Economics, 3, 305-360.
- Jones, G., and George, J. (1998) 'The experience and evolution of trust: Implications for cooperation and teamwork,' Academy of Management Review, 23, 531-546.
- Jones, P., J. Palmer, C. Osterweil and D. Whitehead (1996) Delivering Exceptional Performance, FT Pitman.

- Jones, T.M., and Bowie, N.E. (1998) 'Moral hazards on the road to the "virtual" corporation,' Business Ethics Quarterly, 8, 273-292.
- Kanter, R. (1968) 'Commitment and social organization: a study of commitment in utopian communities,' American Sociological Review, 33, 449-517.
- Kanter, R.M. (1989) When Giants Learn to Dance, New York: Simon and Schuster.
- Katz, D., and Kahn, R.L. (1978) The Social Psychology of Organizations, 2nd edition, New York, Wiley.
- Kelly, S.U., Sung, C., and Farnham, S. (2002) 'Designing for improved social responsibility, user participation and content in on-line communities,' Proceedings of the SIGCHI Conference on Human Factors in Computing Systems, 391-398.
- Klein, H., and Hirschheim, R. (1983) 'Issues and approaches to appraising technological change in the office: a consequentialist perspective,' Office, Technology, and People, 2, 15-42.
- Kotter, J. P. (1988) The Leadership Factor, New York: The Free Press.
- Kotter, J. P., and Heskett, J. L. (1992) Corporate Culture and Performance, New York: Free Press.
- Kramer, R. M. (1999) 'Trust and distrust in organizations: emerging perspectives, enduring questions,' Annual Review of Psychology, 50, 569-598.
- Kramer, Roderick M., and Tyler, Tom, R. (1996) Trust in Organizations: Frontiers of Theory and Research, London, UK: Sage Publications.
- Kreitner, R. (1995) Management, 6th edition, Boston: Houghton Mifflin Company.
- Kuhnert, Karl W., and Lewis, Philip (1987)

'Transactional and transformational leadership: a constructive/developmental analysis,' Academy of Management Review, 12(4), 648-657.

- Lane, C., and Bachmann, R. (1998) Trust Within and Between Organizations, Conceptual Issues and Empirical Applications, Oxford University Press.
- Lane, Christel, and Bachmann, Reinhard (1996) 'The social constitution of trust: supplier relations in Britain and Germany,' Organization Studies, 17(3), 365-395.
- Lewicki, R. J., and Bunker, B. B. (1995) 'Developing and maintaining trust in work relationships', in Kramer, R., and Tyler, T. (eds.) Trust in Organizations: Frontiers of Theory and Research, 114-135, Newbury Park, CA: Sage Publications.
- Lewis, D.J., and Weigert, A. (1985) 'Trust as a social reality', Social Forces, 63, 967-985.
- Lieberson, Stanley, and O'Connor, James, F. (1972) 'Leadership and organizational performance: a study of large corporations', American Sociological Review, 37, 117 -130.
- Lindskold, S. (1978) 'Trust development, the GRIT proposal, and the effects of conciliatory acts on conflict and cooperation.' Psychological Bulletin, 85(4), 772-793.
- Locke, E. A. and Associates (1991) The Essence of Leadership, New York: Lexington Books.
- Locke, E. A., Latham, G. P. (1990) A Theory of Motivation and Task Performance, Englewood Cliffs, NJ: Prentice Hall.
- Lodahl, T. M., Kejner, M. (1965) 'The definition and measurement of job involvement', Journal of Applied Psychology, 49, February, 24-33.
- Lombardo, M. M. and McCall, M. W., Jr. (1978) Leadership: Where Else Can We Go?, Durham, NC: Duke University Press.

- Lowe, K. B., Kroeck, K. G., and Sivasubramaniam, N. (1996) 'Effectiveness correlates of transformational and transactional leadership: a meta-analytic review of the MLQ literature,' Leadership Quarterly, 7, 385-425.
- Ludwig, G. S. (1999) 'Virtual geographic research teams: a case study,' Journal of Geography, 98(3), 149-154.
- Luhmann, N. (1979) Trust and Power, Chichester: John Wiley. Lyng, Johan.
- Luthans, F. (1998) Organizational Behavior, 8th edition, Irwin McGraw-Hill.
- Mamoria, C. B. (1995) Personnel Management, Himalaya Publishing House, Bombay.
- Maslow, A. (1954) Motivation and Personality, New York: Harper.
- Mathieu, J. E., and Zajac, D. M. (1990) 'A review and meta-analysis of the antecedents, correlates, and consequences of organizational commitment,' Psychological Bulletin, 108, 171–194.
- Mayer, R. C., Davis, J. H., and Schoorman, F. D. (1995) 'An integrative model of organizational trust', Academy of Management Review, 20, 709-734.
- McAllister, D. J. (1995) 'Affect and cognition-based trust as foundations for interpersonal cooperation in organizations', Academy of Management Journal, 38, 24-59.
- McFarland, D.E. (1974) Management Principles and Practices, New York, MacMillan.
- McGregor, D. (1960) The Human Side of Enterprise, New York, McGraw Hill.
- McKinlay, A., Proctor, R. and Dunnett, A. (1999) 'An investigation of social loafing and social compensation in computer-supported cooperative work', Proceedings of Group 99, 249-257.

- Meyer, J.P., and Allen, N.J. (1991) 'A three-component conceptualization of organizational commitment,' Human Resource Management Review, 1, 61–89.
- Meyer, J.P., and Allen, N.J. (1997) Commitment in the Workplace: Theory, Research, and Application, Thousand Oaks, CA: Sage Publications.
- Meyer, J.P., Paunonen, S.V. Gellatly, I. R., Goffin, R.D., and Jackson, D.N. (1989) 'Organizational commitment and job performance: it's the nature of the commitment that counts,' Journal of Applied Psychology, 74, 152-156.
- Meyerson, D., Weick, K.E., and Kramer, R.M. (1996) 'Swift trust and temporary groups', in Kramer, R.M., and Tyler, T. (eds.) Trust in Organizations, 166-195, Newbury Park, CA: Sage Publications.
- Miner, J. B. (1975) 'The uncertain future of the leadership concept: An overview,' in Hunt, J. G., and Larson, L. L. (eds.), Leadership Frontiers, 197-208, Kent, OH: Kent State University Press.
- Mintzberg, H. (1973) The Nature of Managerial Work, Englewood Cliffs, NJ: Prentice Hall.
- Mitchell, T.R. and O'Reilly, C. (1983) 'Managing poor performance and productivity in organizations.' In K.M. Rowland and G. Ferris (Eds.), Research in Personnel and Human Resource Management, Vol. 1, JAI Press.
- Moorman, Christine, Zaltman, G., and Deshpande, R. (1992) 'Relationships between providers and users of marketing research: the dynamics of trust within and between organization,' Journal of Marketing Research, 29, August, 314-329.
- Morris, J., and Moberg (1994) 'Work organizations as contexts for trust and betrayal,' in Sarbin, T., and Carney, R.M., Eoyang, C. (Eds), Citizen Espionage: Studies in Trust and Betrayal,163-87, Praeger

Publishers/Greenwood Publishing Group, Westport, CT.

- Morrison, David, E., and Firmstone, J. (2000) 'The social function of trust and implications for e-commerce', International Journal of Advertising, 19 (5), 599-623.
- Mowday, R.T, Porter, W. L, Dubin, R. (1974) 'Unit performance, situational factors and employee attitudes in spatially separated work units', Organizational Behavior and Human Performance, 12(2), 231-248.
- Mowday, R.T., Porter, L. W., and Steers, R. (1982) Organizational Linkages: The Psychology of Commitment, Absenteeism, and Turnover, San Diego, CA: Academic Press.
- Neiderman, F., Beise, C.M., and Beranek, P.M. (1996) 'Issues and concerns about computer-supported meetings: the facilitator's perspective,' MIS Quarterly, 20, 1-22.
- Nicholls, J. (1988) 'The transforming autocrat', Management Today, 114-118.
- Niederman, F., and Beise, C.M. (1999) 'Defining the "virtualness" of groups, teams, and meetings,' Proceedings of the ACM SIGPR Conference on Computer Personnel Research, 14-18.
- Noorderhaven, N. G. (1992) 'Trust and inter-firm relations.' A chapter presented at EAEPE conference, November 4-6, Paris, France.
- O' Connell, S. E. (1998) 'Human communication in the high technology office', Barnett, G. A. (eds.), Handbook of Organizational Communication, 473-482, Ablex Norwood, N.J.
- O'Reilly, C. A., and Chatman, J. (1986) 'Organizational commitment and psychological attachment: the effect of compliance, identification, and internalization on prosocial behavior,' Journal of Applied Psychology, 71, 492–499.

- Olson, G. M., Olson, J. S., Storrsten, M., Carter, M., Herbsleb, J., and Rueter, H. (1993) 'The structure of activity during design meetings,' in Morgan, T., and Carroll, J. (eds.), Design Rationale, Hillsdale, NJ: Erlbaum.
- O'Reilly, Charles (1989) 'Corporations, culture, and commitment: motivation and social control in organizations,' California Management Review, 31, 9-25.
- Orlikoski, W. J., and Robey, D. (1990) 'Information technology and the structuring of organizations,' Information Systems Research, 2, 143-169.
- Orlikowski, W.J. (1992) 'The duality of technology: rethinking the concept of technology in organizations,' Organization Science, 3, 398-427.
- Orlikowski, W.J., Yates, J., Okamura, K., and Fujimoto, M. (1995) 'Shaping electronic communication: the meta-structuring of technology in the context in use,' Organization Science, 6, 423-444.
- Pearce, Jone L., Stevenson, William, B., and Perry, James, L. (1985) 'Managerial compensation based on organizational performance: a time series analysis of the effects of merit pay,' Academy of Management Journal, 28, 261-278.
- Peters, T. and Waterman, R. (1982) In Search of Excellence, New York: Warner Books, Inc.
- Pfeffer, J. (1998) The Human Equation, Boston MA: Harvard Business School Press.
- Pfeffer, Jeffrey, and Salancik, Gerald, R. (1978) The External Control of Organizations: A Resource Dependence Perspective. New York: Harper and Row.
- Pfeffer, Jeffrey. (1994) Competitive Advantage Through People: Unleashing the Power of the Workforce. Boston: Harvard Business School Press.
- Podsakoff, P.M., MacKenzie, S.B., Moorman, R.H.,

and Fetter, R. (1990) 'Transformational leadership behaviors and their effects on followers' trust in leader, satisfaction, and organizational citizenship behaviors', Leadership Quarterly, 1, 107-142.

- Porter, L. and McKibben, L. M. (1988) Management and Development: Drift or Thrust into the 21st Century?, New York: McGraw-Hill.
- Porter, L. W. Lawler, E. E., Hackman, J.R. (1975) Behaviours in Organization, New York, McGraw Hill.
- Porter, L.W., and Lawler, E. E. (1968) Managerial Attitudes and Performance, Homewood, IL: Dorsey Press.
- Porter, L.W., Steers, R. M., Mowday, R.T., and Boulian, P. V. (1974) 'Organizational commitment, job satisfaction, and turnover among psychiatric technicians,' Journal of Applied Psychology, 59, 603–609.
- Porter, M.E. (1985) Competitive Advantage: Creating and Sustaining Superior Performance, New York: Free Press.
- Quick, J.C. (1992) 'Crafting an organizational culture: Herb's hand at Southwest Airlines', Organizational Dynamics, 21 (2), 45-46.
- Rayport, J.F., and Sviokla, J.J. (1995) 'Exploiting the virtual value chain,' Harvard Business Review, 73, 75-85.
- Robbins, S. (1994) Essentials of Organizational Behavior, New Jersey: Prentice- Hall International, Inc.
- Robbins, S. (1996) Organizational Behavior, London: Prentice-Hall International (UK) Limited.
- Rocco, E. (1998) 'Trust breaks down in electronic contexts but can be repaired by some initial face-to-face contact,' Proceedings of the Conference on Human Factors in Computing Systems, 496-502.

- Rousseau, D.M., Sitkin, S.B., Burt, R.S., and Camerer, C. (1998) 'Not so different after all: a cross-discipline view of trust', Academy of Management Review, 23, 393-404.
- Rudman, R. (1998) Performance Planning and Review, Warriewood, Australia: Business and Professional Publishing.
- Saari, L., Johnson, T.R., McLaughlin, S.D. and Zimmerly, D. M. (1988) 'A survey of management education practices in the U.S. companies', Personnel Psychology, 41, 731-743.
- Salancik, G.R., Calder, B.J., Rowland, K.M, Leblebici, H., and Conway, M. (1975) 'Leadership as an outcome of social structure and process: a multidimensional analysis,' in Hunt, J.C., and Larson, L.L. (eds.), Leadership Frontiers, 81-101 Kent, OH: Kent State University Press.
- Salancik, Gerald R., and Pfeffer, J. (1977) 'Constraints on administrator discretion: the limited influence of mayors on city budgets,' Urban Affairs Quarterly, 12, 475 498.
- Samuelson, Bruce A., Galbraith, Craig, S., and McGuire, Joseph, W. (1985) 'Organizational performance and top-management turnover,' Organization Studies, 6, 275-291.
- Sass, J.S., and Canary, D.J. (1991) Organizational commitment and identification: an examination of conceptual and operational convergence, Western Journal of Speech Communication, 55, 275–293.
- Schein, E.H. (1985) Organizational Culture and Leadership, 2nd edition, San Francisco, CA: Jossey-Bass.
- Schein, E.H., (1984) 'Coming to a new awareness of organizational culture,' Sloan Management Review, 25, 3-16.

- Schein, Edgar H. (1992) Organizational Culture and Leadership, 2nd edition, San Francisco: Jossey-Bass Publishers.
- Schneier, C.E. (1974) 'Behaviour modification in management: a review and critique', Academy of Management Journal, 17 (3).
- Seltzer, J., and Bass, B.M (1987) Leadership is More Than Initiation and Consideration, American Psychological Association: New York, NY.
- Shamir, B. (1997) Leadership in Boundaryless Organizations: Disposable or Indisposable, Unpublished manuscript, Hebrew University.
- Shamir, B., and Ben-Ari, E. (1999) 'Leadership in an open army? civilian connections, interorganizational frameworks, and changes in military leadership,' in Hunt, J.G., Dodge, G.E., and Wong, L. (eds.) Out of the Box Leadership: Transforming the 21st Century Army and Other Top Performing Organizations, Stamford, CT: JAI Press.
- Shapiro, D., Sheppard, B., and Cheraskin, L. (1992) 'Business on a handshake,' Negotiation Journal, 8, 365-377.
- Shookla, M.S. (2004) A Handbook of Human Relations with Structured Experiences and Instruments, New Delhi: Macmillan India Ltd.
- Shore, L.M., and Wayne, S. J. (1993) 'Commitment and employee behavior: a comparison of affective commitment and continuance commitment with perceived organizational support', Journal of Applied Psychology, 78, 774-780.
- Siehl, C., and Martin, J. (1990) 'Organizational culture: a key to financial performance?', in Schneider, B. (eds.), Organizational Climate and Culture, 241-281, San Francisco: Jossey-Bass.
- Simms, J. (1997) 'Beauty queen', Marketing Business, 48-51.

- Singh, K. (2000) 'A Study of Work Culture in Selected Indian Organizations', Doctoral Thesis, Faculty of Management Studies, University of Delhi.
- Sinha, J.B.P. (1980) Nurturant Task Leader, New Delhi: Concept Publishing Company.
- Skinner, B.F (1974) About Behaviorism, New York: Random.
- Smirchich, L. (1983) 'Concept of culture and organization analysis,' Administrative Science Quarterly, 28, 339-358.
- Solomon, R. (1996) Ethical Leadership, Emotions and Trust: Beyond Charisma, Kellogg Leadership Studies Project, Center for Political Leadership and Participation, University of Maryland, College Park, MD, 69-90.
- Spears, R., Lea, M., and Lee, S. (1990) 'De-individuation and group polarization in computer-mediated communication,' British Journal of Social Psychology, 29, 121-134.
- Sproull, L., and Kiesler, S. (1991) 'Reducing social context cues: electronic mail in organizational communications,' Management Science, 32, 1492-1512.
- Sreers, R.M. (1977) 'Antecedents and outcomes of organizational commitment,' Administrative Science Quarterly, 22, 46-56.
- Staples, D.S. (1997) The Management of Remote Workers: An Information Technology Perspective, Unpublished Doctoral Thesis, University of Western Ontario, London, Canada.
- Stogdill, R.M. (1974) Handbook of Leadership: A survey of the Literature, New York: Free Press.
- Stoner-Zemel, M.J (1988) 'Visionary leadership, manage-ment, and high performing work units: an

analysis of workers' perceptions', doctoral dissertation, University of Massachusetts, Dissertation Abstracts International, 49, 2307A.

- Strub, P.J., Priest, T.B. (1976) 'Two patterns of establishing trust: the marijuana user', Sociological Focus, 9(4), 399-411.
- Taffinder, P. (1995) The New Leaders: Achieving Corporate Transformation Through Dynamic Leadership, London, Kogan Page.
- Thorlindsson, T. (1987) The Skipper Effect in Icelandic Herring Fishing, University of Iceland, Reykjavik.
- Tvorik, S.J., McGivern, M.H. (1997) 'Determinants of organizational performance', Management Decision, 35(6), 417-435.
- Vroom, V. (1964) Work and Motivation, New York: John Wiley and Sons.
- Wallace, J.E. (1993) 'Professional and organizational commitment: compatible or incompatible?,' Journal of Vocational Behavior, 42, 333-349.
- Walsham, G., and Han, C. (1991) 'Structuration theory and information systems research,' Journal of Applied Systems Analysis, 17, 77 -85.
- Warkentin, M.E., Sayeed, L., and Hightower, R. (1997) 'Virtual teams versus face-to-face teams: an exploratory study of a web-based conference systems,' Decision Sciences, 28 (4), 975-996.
- Weick, K. F. (1990) 'Technology as equivoque: sense making in new techniques,' in Goodman, P.S., Sproull, L. S., and Associates (eds.) Technology and Organizations, 1-44. San Francisco, CA: Jossey-Bass.
- Weiner, Nan (1978) 'Situational and leadership influences on organization performance,' Proceedings of the Academy of Management, 230-234.
- Wellman, B. (1996) 'For a social network analysis

of computer networks: a sociological perspective on collaborative work and virtual community,' Proceedings of the ACM SIGPR/SIGMIS Special Interest Group on Computer Personnel Research Annual Conference, 1-11.

- Wellman, B., Salaff, J., Dimitrova, D., and Garton, L. (1996) 'Computer networks as social networks: collaborative work, telework, and virtual community,' Annual Review of Sociology, 22, 213-238.
- Williamson, O.E. (1991) 'Calculativeness, trust and economic organization', Journal of Law and Economics, 26, 453-486.
- Wood, S., Albanese, M.T. (1995) 'Can we speak of a high commitment management on the shopfloor?', Journal of Management Studies, 32(2), 215-247.
- Yammarino, F.J., and Bass, B.M. (1990) 'Transformational leadership and multiple levels of analysis,' Human Relations, 43(10), 975-995.
- Yammarino, F.J., Spangler, W.D., and Bass, B.M. (1993) 'Transformational leadership and performance: a longitudinal investigation,' Leadership Quarterly, 4(1), 81-102.
- Yates, J., Orlikowski, W.J., and Okamura, K. (1999) 'Explicit and implicit structuring of genres in electronic communication: reinforcement and change of social interaction,' Organization Science, 10, 83-103.
- Yukl, G. (1994) Leadership in Organization, 3rd edition, Prentice Hall, Inc.
- Yukl, G. A. (1989) Leadership in Organizations, 2nd edition, Englewood Cliffs, NJ: Prentice Hall.
- Zand, D. E. (1972) 'Trust and managerial problem solving', Administrative Science Quarterly, 17, 229-239.

- Zheng, J., Veinott, E., Bos, N., Olson, J.S., and Olson, G.M. (2002) 'Trust without touch: jumpstarting long-distance trust with initial social activities,' Proceedings of the SIGCHI Conference on Human Factors in Computing Systems, 141-146.
- Zucker, L. G. (1986) 'Production of trust: institutional sources of economic structure, 1840–1920, Research in Organizational Behavior, 8, 53-111.

Index

N

O

P

R

S